SHRI SHIRDI SAI BABA
Gems from His Philosophical Teachings

Dr. Anitha D.

STERLING PUBLISHERS (P) LTD.
Regd. Office: A1/256 Safdarjung Enclave,
New Delhi-110029. Cin: U22110DL1964PTC211907
Phone: +91 82877 98380
e-mail: mail@sterlingpublishers.in
www.sterlingpublishers.in

SHRI SHIRDI SAIBABA
Gems from His Philosophical Teachings
© 2020, Dr. Anitha D.
ISBN 978 81 944007 3 8

All rights are reserved.
No part of this publication may be reproduced, stored in a retrieval system or transmitted, in any form or by any means, mechanical, photocopying, recording or otherwise, without prior written permission of the original publisher.

Printed and Published in India by

Sterling Publishers Pvt. Ltd.,
Plot No. 13, Ecotech-III, Greater Noida - 201306, U. P. India

Preface

Shri Shirdi Sai Baba is a household name in India and abroad. There are numerous literary works based on the life of the Saint of Shirdi. No one knows the details of his birth and parents. But during and after his lifetime many people were inspired to write about his life and teachings. The foremost and authentic biographical book about him is Shri Sai Satcharita written by Govind Raghunath Dabholkar alias Hemadpant, written in Marathi. The idea of such a biography was conceived during Baba's presence and Baba gave his consent. Hemadpant collected incidents connected to Baba's life, experiences of devotees and also incidents which he had witnessed. The actual work was started and completed after Baba's Mahasamadhi. Since then the Satcharita has been translated to many languages including foreign languages like Nepali, Russian, Malay and so on. This biography is like a formal reference book for any subsequent work authored by anyone. This is true in the present and will be true in future. Though Hemadpant has not written any other book, through this one work his name has become eternally etched in the minds of Sai devotees.

In Shri Sai Satcharita, Hemadpant repeatedly says that it is not he who has written the book, but Baba himself and that he is a mere worker and a puppet. The inspiration, subject matter and writer all are Baba himself. This is true for the books on Baba being written even today. Numerous books have been written on Shri Sai Baba's life by different people. Many of them were writing something for the first time in their life. They were from different walks of life, without any previous literary background.

Why are so many books written on the life of a fakir who lived in an old, dilapidated masjid in a remote village? In Satcharita Hemadpant says, 'The life story of Sai is like a vast ocean – endless, inexhaustible and full of jewels. The life of Sai is profound. It is impossible to describe it fully.' Shri Sai Satcharita is written in ovi metre and contains 53 chapters, with more than 9,000 verses. Each chapter is a mixture of philosophical truths, stories and moral advice. As Hemadpant said, 'Shri Sai Baba's biography is an inexhaustible mine of spiritual wealth.' Baba himself says, 'My treasury is overflowing. Whoever wants to take it, can come and dig it and take away cartful of wealth.' By this what Baba meant was that whoever wants, can freely take any amount of spiritual benefits or divine knowledge from him.

We all need to study, meditate, contemplate and follow Baba's teachings. Once we develop an internal bond with Baba and nurture good qualities and piety, he will impart divine knowledge to us. But we have to do the necessary efforts of digging. Digging in this context means leading a virtuous life, taking interest in the spiritual ways of life, deeply thinking about purpose of human life and avoiding all vices. If we practise all these, Baba will stay with us and lead us to our final destination.

The goal of human life is to have a desireless mental state while leading an active life. We should realise the unity among ourselves, our fellow human beings and the Universal Soul. Once we attain the real knowledge, we will be able to give up this visible world as if it was a blade of grass. But because of the latent tendencies of many past lifetimes and conditioning by internal and external factors, it is not possible for common people to achieve such a state easily. We should at least strive for the right thinking and right behaviour. In chapter 8 of Satcharita, Hemadpant says:

> If the whole life is spent in these four ways – eating, sleeping, being constantly afraid and indulging in sex – then what would be the difference between the human and an animal? Oh, you decide using your discretion.
>
> Chapter 8, verse 13

Preface

Hemadpant says that the human body and human life are superior to other forms of life and we are created for a special purpose – for acquiring the knowledge of the Supreme, because only a human being has a discerning mind. The sharp and intelligent human being can understand that this splendid visible world is a sport (Maya) of the Paramatman and realise the glory and power of that real controller. But human beings are using their precious body for sensual enjoyment and amassing money. When people lead such degraded existence, saints, who are the embodiment of knowledge, bliss, universal love and detachment, manifest on earth.

Through their way of life and their teachings, saints show us the proper way of leading our lives. What is needed from us is an interest in listening to their stories, which will transform us internally. Spiritual experiences are subtle and very personal. They cannot be described adequately by words, just like our tongue can taste sweetness but we cannot describe the taste. All persons have to experience it by themselves. Others can only help. In the same manner, I am unable to explain the divine experiences I had with Shri Shirdi Sai Baba. Like other devotees, I also recognise Baba as an avatar of Lord Dattatreya, the Jagad Guru and a godly figure who is very near to us. When I thought of translating Shri Sai Satcharita to Malayalam, Baba himself took over the task. When I had a wish to compile the philosophical truths and moral lessons which are embedded in Shri Sai Satcharita, Baba himself presented the invaluable gems to me. Like a humble worker, I have merely presented them.

May the incomparable light from these invaluable gems brighten your heart!

Dr. Anitha D.

*****

Contents

Preface		*iii*
Introduction		1
1.	Faith	11
2.	Ignorance	25
3.	Attachment	37
4.	Greed	47
5.	Enmity	57
6.	Sense Control	66
7.	Dispassion	77
8.	Devotion	86
9.	Love	100
10.	Truthfulness	111
11.	Humility	122
12.	Courage	131
13.	Chanting of God's Name	142
14.	Study of Holy Texts	150
15.	Company of Saints	160
16.	Purity	172
17.	Guru's Greatness	183
18.	Discipleship	197
Bibliography		*208*

INTRODUCTION

Shri Shirdi Sai Baba is worshipped as God by millions of people. His teachings are about universal love, non-violence and God consciousness. His mission was to remind the humankind about the existence of God and direct people towards that goal. He told his devotees to be loyal to God and depend on only God.

He described himself as a servant of God. 'Allah Malik', or God is the owner, was his japa. He said:

> In this world, everybody has somebody or the other, but nobody belongs to me. Allah and only Allah is mine.
>
> Chapter 14, verse 94

> The only true giver is my Sarkar. Can anyone else be compared with him? How can the finite be the ornament of the infinite?
>
> Chapter 32, verse 160

> The skill of my Fakir, the leela of my Bhagavan, the aptitude of my Sarkar is quite unique.
>
> Chapter 32, verse 165

Baba wants His followers to lead a life of devotion and God consciousness. At the same time, He recognises the fact that most people are unenlightened and immersed in animals-like activities. So it is difficult for them to follow the path of knowledge and reach the destination, that is, Brahman. For all these people, he advised the path of bhakti or devotion. Devotion to the guru or God will not occur unless one is pure at heart. Mental purity is achieved by selfless love. When you transcend the ideas of 'I' and 'mine', then only you can see that God pervades nature and sustains each and every creature. The feeling of oneness develops by listening to and imbibing the teachings of saints and obtaining their grace by pure devotion and service. Saints are the mines of divine knowledge. To acquire that treasure you must be qualified according to the standards set by them. The standards are strict and well-set, mental purity being the foremost. Baba says:

> My treasury is full, I can give anything anyone asks for, but I have to take into account the receiver's capacity. I give that which one is able to receive only.
>
> Chapter 17, verse 78
>
> I say dig up this wealth and plunder cartloads of it. The blessed son of a true mother should fill his store with this wealth.
>
> Chapter 32, verse 163

Hemadpant says:

> Those who receive his grace become inconceivably powerful, for they receive the treasure of self-bliss and discrimination together with knowledge.
>
> Chapter 30, verse 7

The meaning of this verse is that a person who is graced by a saint gains divine knowledge, ability to discriminate between the real and unreal and he rejoices in his own self. Thus, he becomes powerful enough to overcome the mundane existence and realise the Paramatman.

Introduction

The most valuable and desirable treasure human beings can obtain is self-knowledge. This knowledge is usually hidden by the body-mind-intellect. But it will shine through and reveal itself when we receive the grace of a saint. Then worldly existence becomes a joyful play, not a tragic drama to be undergone miserably. So how can we obtain this treasure? Chapters 16 and 17 of the Satcharita contain the advice given by Baba to a wealthy miser who came seeking knowledge of Brahman or self- knowledge. Baba told him about who is eligible to acquire knowledge of Brahman and how to obtain it. Baba said that people who seek worldly benefits are plenty in number, but nobody asks for Brahman, which is the real knowledge and that he is eager to get such devotees who are looking for Brahman. Then he described the splendour of Brahman:

The sun and the moon rise and set regularly. Gods like Indra and the kings reign over their kingdoms properly and protect their subjects. Brahman is the root cause for all this. When its minuteness is considered, the Atman is microscopic, smaller than an atom. When its largeness is considered, the Atman is larger than the biggest immense. But all this comparison is subjective because the Atman is beyond any unit of measure. Thus, the size and shape are only for namesake. The Atman is complete in itself without any distinguishable property. The Atman is not born, nor does it die. There is no root cause for it. It is unborn, permanent, everlasting, ancient and not easy to comprehend. Brahman can be seen in the representation of 'aum' and that is its entire nature. Brahman is difficult to achieve even for yogis who have mastered reaching samadhi and coming out of it, then can it be possible or accessible to all? In the effort to ascertain its nature, the Vedas were exhausted, the ascetics became forest dwellers, the Upanishads gave up – thus nobody was ever able to analyse and ascertain it.

Baba then says that only with the grace of a sadguru can one attain Brahman. He describes the result and fruits of attaining Brahman:

> As soon as the mind wavers with respect to the Supreme Self, all the passions and senses become active, but when the mind is steadfast in self-realisation, then the passions weaken. He who has turned away from his real self, find all material pleasures always confronting him; but if he turns to his real self, the same objects hold no attraction. 'I am that Brahman', when this is realised, then he who has realised it surrenders to the Supreme Self. And for him the illusion of the existence of the universe disappears. When there is true knowledge of the self, the person's entire nature becomes one with Brahman and the world turns into ashes. That false knowledge, which is motivated for the sake of fulfilment of desire, will disappear and truth, pure consciousness and bliss will stabilise. The state of self-realisation will arise. The other word for this is liberation.

Baba says that unless one attains self-knowledge, the person will be subjected to the cycle of births and deaths.

Baba told the person, who was not ready to part with even five rupees, that the path of knowledge of Brahman was difficult and not easy to follow for anyone, but to a fortunate person it manifests itself. Only the aspirants of the highest category can attain the knowledge of Brahman flawlessly. Mediocre aspirants are bound by traditions and follow the steps of rituals according to the shastras. They progress stage-by-stage. But for an incapable person, the whole effort about Brahman was useless.

Baba then explained the prerequisites and means for attaining Brahman or Brahmajnanam. They are:

1. *Surrender of the five pranas, the five senses of action and perception, ego, intellect and mind*

   Pranas indicate the life-force (wind) moving in a subtle plane (pranamayakosa) through the physical body frame (annamayakosa). Pranas are essentially of the nature of energy. Depending on the sites of distribution, the life-force is divided into five kinds, that is, one primary prana is divided into five according to their movement and direction. They are:

   Prana: It governs the intake of substances. It is the forward moving air. It moves inward and governs the ingestion of all things – eating, drinking, inhalation and reception of sensory impressions as well as mental experiences

   Samana: It governs the digestion of food. It is the balancing air. It moves from the periphery to the centre. It aids in digestion, helps in absorption of oxygen in the breath and homogenises and absorbs experiences, whether sensory, emotional or mental.

   Vyana: It governs the circulation of nutrients. It is the outward moving air. It moves from centre to the periphery. It governs circulation at all levels. It moves the food, water and oxygen throughout the body, keeps our emotions and thoughts circulating in the mind and imparts strength and movement.

   Udana: It governs the positive energy. It is the upward moving air. It governs the growth of the body, the ability to stand, speak, make effort, enthusiasm and our will.

   Apana: It governs the elimination of waste materials. It is the air that moves away. It governs all forms of elimination and reproduction – elimination of the stool and urine, expelling the semen, menstrual fluids and foetus as well as the elimination of negative sensory and emotional and mental experiences.

The five organs of sensory perception are the eyes, ears, tongue, nose and skin. The five organs of action are speech, arms, legs, anus and genitalia. Mind is the inner subtle faculty of perception and thinking. Ego is the feeling of 'I'. Intellect is the discriminating faculty.

To denote the five pranas and the five sensory organs of perception and action, Baba asked for a loan of five rupees.

Unless we control our vitals, senses, mind, body and actions, we can never enter the realm of Brahmajnanam, even in our dreams.

What does Baba mean by wanting us to surrender all the gross and subtle faculties? He implies that we should control our urges and desires and direct our movements, thoughts and ideas towards the acquisition of self-knowledge.

2. *Self- control and detachment*

To gain self-knowledge, we should control our physical and mental demands. We should be mentally detached from the ideas of 'I' and 'mine', we should be egoless. We should not have attachment to our own body, spouse, children, wealth, material possessions, status and so on. We should be desireless in every walk of life and our only goal must be self-realisation.

3. *Discrimination*

We should be able to discriminate between what is pleasurable and what is good for our spiritual progress, shun the pleasures and accept the good. We should think about the unreal and illusory nature of visible world and the permanency and reality of the Paramatman.

4. *Sharp and penetrating intelligence*

A clear intellect is essential for a seeker.

5. Steady mind

We should always keep our mind calm and contented. A person who is tormented by the three-fold calamities (tridosha) is not fit for seeking Brahman. The three-fold calamities are aadhyatmic (spiritual trouble), aadibhowdik (materialistic trouble) and aadidaivik (destined trouble). The body, with its organs and the life in them, is subjected to troubles originating from birth, life and death. All bodily diseases and pains, whether congenital or acquired, originate from spiritual trouble. Materialistic trouble occurs from people and objects with which a person comes in contact, including natural calamities. Destined troubles are those troubles which we will have to endure, based on our actions. A seeker should remain balanced in all conditions and be able to face any trouble.

6. Mental purity

Mental purity is the foremost prerequisite. A seeker should remove all ignorance–delusions like greed, anger, attachment, passion, pride, hope, desire, covetousness, malice, avarice and enmity.

7. Fearlessness

A seeker should be courageous and without fear.

8. Unwavering faith and belief in the existence of Brahman

Faith is the foundation upon which devotion to the guru or Brahman to be developed.

9. Ability to concentrate deeply

Seekers should be able to avoid distractions and concentrate on the goal. For that, we have to master our body, mind and impulses.

10. Diligence and practice

Seekers should perform the prescribed duties and routines consistently. They should follow the daily routines, as well as those occurring occasionally and those prescribed by the shastras. They should always follow the teachings of the holy scriptures and their guru.

11. *Nonduality*

Seekers should see themselves and all beings as equal and the same. They should be above the dualities of happiness and miseries, virtuous and sinful. They should see themselves, others and Brahman as one. They should have the unwavering belief that 'I am that'.

12. *Abstinence from forbidden, low and sinful actions*

A seeker should always behave and act according to the codes of ethics and morality.

13. *Eagerness*

A seeker should constantly consider how to get released from the bondages of this illusory, visible world and be eager to attain the real knowledge.

14. *Liking for solitude*

A seeker should cultivate liking for solitude so that he can gather his energy and time to engage in spiritual ways of life. Such a person should not engage in arguments and discussions.

15. *Non-doership*

Seekers should not be attached to the fruits of their actions. They should believe that their duty is only to act according to the code of conduct which governs them.

16. *Holy company*

Seekers should obtain company of holy people, that is, satsang. They should have faith in the holy people, obedience and readiness to imbibe their teachings and diligently bring them into action.

Introduction

17. *Reading, study and contemplation of holy religious texts*

Holy texts are guides for virtuous living. They act as a teacher, friend and relative. A seeker should study them regularly and meditate on their teachings.

18. *God's grace*

Seekers should nurture devotion to God. They should concentrate, meditate and contemplate on God. They should mould their thinking and actions to direct them to devotional ways.

19. *Guru's grace*

Without our guru's help, without a sadguru's grace, we cannot know what Brahman is. By sadguru's grace the impossible becomes possible. When we become fit and suitable by leading our life as based on the qualities mentioned so far, we get sadguru's grace.

20. *Adherence to guru's teachings and practice*

Seekers should continue to practise their rituals and studies even after they get the knowledge. They should be loyal and obedient to their guru and the guru's teachings, whether they are with the guru or away.

These teachings can be summarised as follows:

As a devotee or a seeker or a disciple, we should have faith in our guru and God. We should know what is ignorance and remove all delusions like greed, anger, passions, pride, enmity and so on. We should have self-control and should not have attachment to anything worldly. We should have dispassion and devotion and seek our guru's grace. We should have universal love, truthfulness, humility, mental purity, equanimity and courage. We should obtain our guru's grace by constant remembrance (naamajapa, or constant chanting of guru's and God's names), satsang and study of holy texts. We should completely surrender to the sadguru by practising perfect discipleship.

I have based this book on the abstract concepts described in the Satcharita. The first chapter is on faith, the foundation for receiving grace. Then, I discuss the hindrances in attaining self-realisation, like ignorance (ajnanam), attachment, greed and enmity. This is followed by listing the qualities to be nurtured like sense control, dispassion, devotion (bhakti), love, truthfulness, humility, courage, purity, chanting of God's name (naamajapa), study of holy texts and satsang. Lastly, I have described the guru's greatness and perfect discipleship.

This book is not a complete compilation of all the concepts described in the Satcharita. This is a humble endeavour to describe some of the gems. Holy texts *Shri Gurucharitra, Tripurarahasyam, Jnaneswari, Yoga Vasishta, Dasabodha, Viveka Chudamani, Bhagavatapuranam* and *Devi Mahatmyam* helped me to grasp the subtle philosophical concepts described in the Satcharita. Each chapter in this book contains the verses, stories and incidents relevant to the particular abstract concept adapted from the Satcharita. I have mentioned stories from the Puranas and other holy texts as relevant to the context.

This is a small and simple effort from me to help devotees approach the Satcharita more sincerely and gravely, with an insight and get full benefit from its reading and study. Faults and flaws will definitely be there, but leaving the sense of doership, I dedicate this humble work at the holy feet of Shri Sai Baba.

FAITH

I do not need elaborate worship either sixteen-fold or eight-fold. Where there is infinite faith, I reside there.

Chapter 13, verse 13

Sacred mantras, the tirthas, the deity, the brahmin, the fortune-teller and the druggists – thus the seventh in this line is the guru – all these need faith.

Chapter 8, verse 81

Success is achieved in proportion to the faith in all these. Depending upon the intentness of the mind, success varies.

Chapter 8, verse 82

When one wishes to cross the ocean, one must have faith in the navigator; similarly, to cross the samsaric ocean, one must have faith in the guru.

Chapter 10, verse 7

The handle of the grinding stone often has to be moved about to fix it firmly. Similarly is the case with faith at the guru's feet. Sai strengthens it by testing it.

Chapter 29, verse 123

When he sees the faith and devotion of the devotee, he gives the wealth of happiness due to moksha in the palm of the hands, most easily.

Chapter 10, verse 8

1

FAITH
(Shraddha)

The spiritual goal of life (paramartha) is certain for him who has the pure strength of faith, together with the powerful strength of knowledge, added to steadfast patience.

Chapter 23, verse 192

Faith is the complete trust or confidence in someone or something, is the meaning in the dictionary. Faith has another meaning also. It is a strong belief in the doctrines of a religion, based on a spiritual conviction rather than proof. In other words, faith is a strongly held belief in spite of absence of any concrete proofs.

Faith is not an emotion or a feeling. Emotions are physical or instinctive reactions to an external event or situation. Feelings are mental associations and reactions to an emotion. But faith is an inner conviction that we can solely depend on someone or something. For human beings this develops first towards the mother, because the mother provides security, protection and support. As time passes this extends to other family members also. Once the child reaches school, he or she develops faith in the teachers and peers. Upon marriage, the couple has mutual faith in each other. They develop faith in their children and vice versa. Outside the family, they have faith in relatives, neighbours, community and religious leaders. This type of faith, that is, faith between fellow human beings needs a secure base. In this type of faith, we need to be cautious and discriminative, because if we put faith in an unworthy person, we will be deceived. Faith between human beings is seldom stable. It fluctuates with external conditions. Sometimes it becomes stronger, sometimes weaker and sometimes it is lost. Apart from fellow human beings, we have to put faith in time and nature also, like a farmer sowing the field or a person waiting eagerly for a good turn of events.

Faith in Spirituality
In spirituality, faith has a totally different application. When a person cannot find a secure base within himself or herself or in fellow beings, the person turns to a higher level. This higher level could be in the form of a scripture or a godly figure. The godly figure can be personal (with a form) or impersonal (formless). Humans place faith in these entities and depend on them for strength and hope. Since the whole universe is in the form of energy and intelligence, all the objects in it will be of the same nature. But in these objects, the level of energy and intelligence vary because of the conditioning. So they are not able to fully identify with the higher levels. But persistent and strong faith confer on them some of the higher qualities by which they will be able to endure life's problems and find solutions.

But is it possible to keep faith consistently over a long period? It is not easy to keep firm faith. Impatience and doubt will invariably overpower a person's resolve. In the Puranas we can observe many such occasions. When Vinatha was impatient to have a son, she broke open one of the two eggs given by her husband, Sage Kashyapa. She could not wait till the stipulated period was over. From the broken egg, a half-matured being came out and he cursed his mother to be a servant of her co-wife. Gandhari was impatient to have her own children after knowing that Kunti had given birth to a son. She kicked her own abdomen and a homogenous fleshy mass was expelled from her uterus. The mass was cut into a hundred pieces by Sage Vyas and incubated. Evil Kauravas were born from those pieces. Dronacharya knew well that his son Aswathama was immortal. But when he heard Yudhishtara's words, doubts crept into his mind, he succumbed to grief and Dhrishtadhyumna killed him. On the contrary, in spite of all the trials and tribulations, Pandavas placed firm faith in Lord Krishna and the Lord always protected them. In the royal assembly hall, Dussasana tried to remove Draupadi's dress and disrobe her. Draupadi called Lord Krishna with such an intense faith and surrender that Lord materialised an inexhaustible store of dress on her body so that Dussasana fell exhausted and his evil intention could not be implemented. Thus, faith is complemented by other essentials like patience, strong conviction and unconditional surrender.

Faith is such an essential quality that Lord Krishna, holy people, yogis and prophets have all stressed its importance. 'You maintain your faith, do your duties diligently, wait patiently and you will get the result' – this is the advice and assurance given by them. Shri Shirdi Sai Baba advised people to keep faith in their respective belief systems, gurus, deities and scriptures. To those people who took refuge in him, he advised them to place all their problems and burdens on him, to put faith in his words and wait patiently. Baba advised that a disciple should have firm faith in the guru and should not strive for any mantra or upadesa from the guru. He told Radhabai Desmukh, who came to Shirdi and decided to fast until Baba gave her a mantra, about his own guru:

> In the beginning he had my head shaved and asked for only two pice, which I gave immediately. I ardently prayed for him to give me those magical words of a mantra.
>
> Chapter 19, verse 49
>
> Faith (shraddha) and patience (saburi) – these were the two pice, nothing else. I gave him immediately, by which my guru was pleased with me, who was like my mother.
>
> Chapter 19, verse 52
>
> Though the guru is very powerful, he expects only wisdom from his disciple, firm faith, lots of courage and patience at the feet of the guru.
>
> Chapter 19, verse 58

The disciple or devotee should have firm faith in the guru and should diligently continue to serve and wait patiently. Faith should be kept on the unshakable foundation of patience. Along with that, the disciple should continuously remember the guru. The all-knowing guru will nourish the disciple with glances, like a mother tortoise. Baba advised the lady about the virtue of patience:

> The valour of human beings lies in being patient. It wards off the sins, worries and miseries. The difficulties are cleared in some ways or the other and fear and panic vanish.
>
> Chapter 19, verse 54
>
> Patience gains success ultimately. Difficulties run off helter-skelter. Thorn of evil thoughts have no scope.
>
> Chapter 19, verse 55

Patience is a mine of virtues. She is the queen of pious thinking. Faith and she are true sisters and they dearly love each other.

Chapter 19, verse 56

A human being without patience becomes miserable. He may be a scholar or a virtuous person, but life without it is futile.

Chapter 19, verse 57

Faith and patience are the grindstones against which a disciple's worth is valued.

Just as a stone and a gem, if both are rubbed against a grindstone, both shine – but a stone is a stone and a gem, after all, is a lustrous and precious stone.

Chapter 19, verse 59

Both undergo the same process of polishing. But can a stone shine like a gem? A gem may become a luminous diamond, but the stone will remain the same, only it will become a little smoother.

Chapter 19, verse 60

A virtuous disciple will shine like a diamond, if he cultivates the qualities of faith and patience. The weak-hearted will remain as before or may have a little progress. Their achievement in spirituality will be in proportion to the faith in their guru and willingness to patiently wait till the period decided by the guru.

Most of people who came to Baba were eager for solutions for their mundane problems. Unless the material life is stable, a common person can never think of spirituality. Even if the material existence is comfortable, only a few people will be inclined to follow the spiritual ways. When a crisis that appears to be insurmountable occurs and is overcome, some people may develop discriminative thinking which makes them turn to the spiritual path. When people went to Baba with their immediate, mundane problems, Baba relieved them of their troubles, so that they could be contented in life. Once they were stable, their minds could be inclined towards God and godly ways. The jolt that occurred in their lives like disease, loss, financial problem, etc., could act as a catalyst for developing detachment and discrimination. So when such common folks approached him with their mundane problems, Baba gave them lessons of faith and patience also. Baba gave them what appeared to be queer instructions and remedies. Those who put faith in Baba's words and acted accordingly were relieved of their problems. Others had to face calamities. In Satcharita there are accounts of many devotees who put implicit faith in Baba's words. There are also stories about others who wavered in their resolve and suffered.

Bhimaji Patil

In the 13th chapter there is description of Bhimaji Patil who was afflicted with tuberculosis. No medicines could cure him. He tried all conventional and unconventional remedies. Finally, with Chandorkar's help, he reached Shirdi and prayed pitifully to Baba. Baba comforted him with his merciful glances and words. Baba told him to stay at Bhimabai's house and assured him that he would be relieved of the illness within a couple of days. Baba gave him Udi and rubbed some of it on his forehead as well. Immediately, Bhimaji felt well and he could start walking. When he reached Bhimabai's house, he saw that it was a small place.

The floor had just been thumped smooth with the help of a wooden log, for the purpose of levelling. Therefore it was wet. Even then he obeyed Baba's orders.

Chapter 13, verse 161

He would have got a dry place in the village, since Bhimaji had many contacts. But Baba had particularly indicated the place, so he did not think of going anywhere else.

Chapter 13, verse 162

He spread out two gunny bags upon the floor, on top of which he spread out his bedding. Patil went to sleep peacefully.

Chapter 13, verse 163

This devotee had implicitly put his faith in Baba and did not think of the adequacy or convenience of the place. As per our modern medicine, a cramped and wet place is unsuitable for patients suffering from tuberculosis. But a saint's words are all-powerful. Bhimaji was cured of the illness by two dreams.

Bala Ganapat

This devotee was a tailor. He was a great devotee of Baba. Once he was suffering from malaria. He came to Baba and prayed for relief from the fever. Baba gave him the following advice:

Feed a few morsels of curd and rice to a black dog near the temple of Mother Lakshmi. You will be cured immediately.

Chapter 13, verse 92

Bala Ganapat went home and found some leftover rice and a little curd. Bala wondered whether he would find a black dog near the temple. But when he reached there, he saw a black dog approaching him, wagging its tail. He was happy and fed the dog the curd and rice he had brought. Later, he informed Baba also. The whole incident may seem very strange, but Bala recovered and was cured of the malaria. The devotee put his entire faith in Baba's words and acted without evaluating whether it made sense to him or not.

Buti

Once the devotee Buti suffered from cholera. He was in distress and had intense thirst due to simultaneously vomiting and passing motions. Dr Pillai did whatever he could, but there was no relief. So he approached Baba. Baba told him, 'Give him an infusion of milk boiled with almonds, walnuts and pistachios. This will quench his thirst and the disease will be cured immediately.' Buti was given this infusion to drink and his disease disappeared. Walnuts, pistachios and almonds –will they ever give relief from cholera? For the devotees who worshipped Baba as Parabrahman, his words were their medicine.

Madhavrao (Shama)

Madhavrao was a great devotee and Baba's helper. One day he was bitten on his little finger by a snake. His condition was grave but still he refused to be taken to the Vithoba temple. The villagers always took snake-bite victims to the Vithoba temple because they believed only Vithoba could cure them. But Shama refused to go there and went to the masjid instead. He put his faith in the Udi and Baba even in such a critical situation. Baba ordered the poison not to climb up into the body. Baba's words provided the cure and Shama was saved.

When a devotee or a disciple depends on the guru with unshakable faith and firmly believes there is no other refuge, then the guru takes over the burden.

Now let us observe the experience of a devotee who wavered in his faith.

Amir Shakkar

Amir was working as a broker. He lived in Korhale. He had arthritis, which affected the joints of the body. When he was unable to get cured, he left his business and came to Shirdi, bowed down at the feet of Baba and prayed for a cure for his illness. Baba told him to stay in the chavadi. He was not allowed to go even to the masjid. The place where he had to stay was not suitable at all for the illness according to medical belief.

The chavadi was an old and dilapidated building. The floor was uneven where chameleons, lizards, scorpions and snakes roamed freely.

Chapter 22, verse 118

Besides, lepers and other diseased persons lived there. Dogs roamed around eating leftover food. Amir was very troubled but he could not say anything to Baba.

Chapter 22, verse 119

At the rear side, there was a knee-deep heap of garbage. There were a number of burrows made by serpents and scorpions, in the backyard. He was in a wretched condition and it was a real ordeal of a lifetime for him.

Chapter 22, verse 120

Faith

It rained from above and below the ground was wet. The place was uneven. Cold breeze blew through it. Amir was very worried.

Chapter 22, verse 121

All the joints in his body were stiff. The place was wet and windy. It was an extremely wet place. But Baba's words served as the medicine.

Chapter 22, verse 122

Rain, wind or wet; the ground rough, uneven or pitted – all this was not to be considered, as Baba told him to live there.

Chapter 22, verse 123

Believing Baba's words were medicine, Amir stayed there. In the morning and evening he had Baba's darshan. Besides, every alternate day, Baba used to stay in the chavadi.

After some time, Amir felt that to stay in one place for such a long time was like an imprisonment or a bondage. So one night he left the place and went to a dharmashala in Kopergaon. There he saw a fakir who was about to die. The fakir asked for some water and he gave it to him. But as soon as the fakir drank it, he fell down, lifeless. Fearing that he would be held responsible for the fakir's death, Amir ran back to Shirdi the same night itself. He gave up the wrong path and obeyed Baba's words. His faith bore fruit and he was cured of his illness.

From Amir's story, we can see that when conditions are unfavourable or challenging, it becomes extremely difficult to keep faith. But we have to keep faith under all kinds of trying circumstances and conditions and wait patiently. At the same time, we should continue to perform the necessary actions and efforts. Then definitely Baba's compassion will work for our benefit.

Once, a well-to-do gentleman from Bombay, Harish Chandra Pitale, brought his sick son to Shirdi. The boy was suffering from epilepsy and none of the treatment had been effective. As a last resort, he sought Baba's darshan. The boy was placed at Baba's feet. As soon as the boy's eyes met Baba's, the boy fell unconscious and he had a severe attack of epilepsy. It appeared that the boy was about to die. The mother started lamenting loudly. Baba consoled her and assured her that within half-an-hour the boy would regain consciousness. As per Baba's instructions, they took him to the lodging house and immediately the boy came to his senses. The parents were overjoyed. They came back for Baba's darshan and expressed their gratitude. Then Baba asked them:

> Have the waves of doubts and desires ebbed now?
> Shri Hari will protect him who has faith and patience.
>
> Chapter 26, verse 83

From all these incidents, we can conclude that faith should be exercised with full inner conviction, leaving aside all doubts, apprehensions, prejudices and expectations. We should be willing to endure any hardships. When the path seems to be full of thorns and ditches, we should keep our faith in Baba, follow his teachings strictly and wait patiently for his grace to work. Definitely, Baba's grace will solve our problems. In chapter 29, Hemadpant says:

> As one goes along the directed path, in the beginning everything seems to go well. Later, thorny shrubs seem to be so spread out that one encounters thorns only in all quarters.
>
> Chapter 29, verse 125

> Then one's faith is shaken and doubts easily arise. 'Why has Sai brought me to this difficult path?' one could ask.
>
> Chapter 29, verse 126

When one feels like this, make a strong effort to hold on to your faith. These difficulties are there to test you; then only will firm faith becomes a part of you.

Chapter 29, verse 127

Facing these difficulties and constantly chanting Sai's name, all the problems will be removed. This is the tremendous power of the name.

Chapter 29, verse 128

That is the purpose of these difficulties, which are also created by Sai. It is only then that one remembers Sai and chants his name, which brings about the end of all the difficulties.

Chapter 29, verse 129

So whatever be the external conditions, we should have unshakable faith and patience. When a devotee or disciple has such steadfast faith, wonders can happen through the guru's mercy – a dry wood will turn into a live tree with flowers and fruits. In *Shri Gurucharitra*, there is an account of a devotee Narahari. This devotee was afflicted with leprosy. His body became deformed and became ugly. All his relations abandoned him. He sought refuge at Shri Guru Shri Narasimhasaraswathi. Shri Guru asked him to take a dry udumbara wood which was brought there by a man. Shri Guru asked him to go to the sangamam (confluence) of Bhima–Amaraja rivers. He should plant the dry wood there and water it three times a day. Shri Guru told him that when the dry wood produced leaves and flowers, then his leprosy would be cured.

Narahari devotedly followed Shri Guru's command. He did pooja and abhisheka to the wood three times a day, observing a strict fast. Seven days passed like this. Villagers ridiculed him and tried to stop him. But he did not heed to their words. He told them that his only aim was to strictly obey Shri Guru's words, whether he died or lived, it did not matter. The people went to Shri Guru and requested him to do something to dissuade Narahari. Shri Guru went to the sangamam and saw that the brahmin was doing pooja and pouring water on the dry log. Seeing Narahari's firm faith, Shri Guru took some water and sprinkled it over the log. Immediately, the log changed into a live tree with green shoots and flowers. Along with that, Narahari's leprosy also was cured and he had a new, radiant body. Shri Guru told the villagers, 'One's objectives are fulfilled according to one's faith and belief.'

Conclusion

Baba's devotees should cultivate firm, unshakable faith in his words. Along with that they should also have patience, practise his teachings, remember him constantly and have complete surrender and obedience. Then they can overcome all worries and problems and will be able to follow the spiritual path. Ultimately, when the time is ripe, Baba will help them realise the real knowledge

IGNORANCE

He who is concentrated on riches and fame and yet craving for sense enjoyment in spite of having had it and is incessantly thinking of wife and children, his knowledge is nothing but ignorance.

Chapter 50, verse 81

Thus one who is obsessed with wealth, sons and wife does not know his well-being even though he may be knowledgeable. Therefore so long as he is without devotion, his knowledge is veiled by ignorance.

Chapter 50, verse 82

False knowledge or illusion are existing from the very beginning. They are like the futile illusions created by the silver of the oyster shell and water of the mirage. They should be considered as erroneous conceptions and obstacles and therefore should be removed.

Chapter 17, verse 19

When the illusion is removed, similar is the state of mind of the human beings. The rope, the ray of the sun and the mother-of-pearl shell – the illusion that they are different is removed immediately.

Chapter 16, verse 84

This is all due to reciprocal attraction between the viewer and the things viewed. Light the lamp of knowledge and wash away the impurities of ignorance. This will annihilate illusions.

Chapter 16, verse 86

IGNORANCE
Ajnanam

This material world is full of ignorance. It is based and flourishes on ignorance. Understand that salvation is not possible without true knowledge.

Chapter 16, verse 149

The word 'jnanam' means knowledge. Its opposite is 'ajnanam' which means ignorance. That which is not knowledge is ajnanam. The meaning of 'ignorance' in the dictionary is given as lack of knowledge, understanding or information of something. We see in our day-to-day lives how we have to face many problems if we are ignorant of the matters which we are supposed to know. If we do not know how to earn a livelihood, we and our dependents will live in poverty. If we are ignorant of the ways of the society in which we live, others will create many problems and challenges for us. If we do not know the prevailing laws and follow them, the authorities will impose fines or punish us. So it is evident how harmful it is to be ignorant of mundane ways of life.

In the spiritual sense, ignorance or ajnanam means the lack of real knowledge. What is real knowledge? Real knowledge is the realisation of our own self and its unity with the Universal Soul. Real knowledge is the realisation of the illusory nature of the visible world and the realisation of the reality of the Paramatman and its supremacy. When we are ignorant of our real nature, we get immersed in the mundane ocean of sorrows and sufferings. We get sucked into the cycle of repeated births and deaths.

Our real nature is pure consciousness which is a part-and-parcel of the Universal Consciousness. Real knowledge or jnanam is understanding the light or living presence in our own body. According to Satcharita, that which masks the living presence is called ajnanam. Baba repeatedly affirms that the goal of human life is to live in God consciousness or to live in the light and purity of the Paramatman.

The same light shines and pervades the whole visible world. It resides inside every creature. So the Paramatman, the visible world and all the creatures are essentially one and the same. Ajnanam is the veil which prevents the light of this knowledge, that is, jnanam, from spreading. The veil or ajnanam is the illusions created by senses and the mind. Sensory perceptions are defective and limited. Hemadpant describes illusion by giving examples of the oyster shell, rope and mirage. In bright sunlight, oyster shell may be wrongly believed to be silver. In dim light a rope may appear as a garland or a snake or a stick. A mirage is an optical illusion perceived by a traveller in a desert. In this, the reflected rays of sunlight appear to be water to the traveller.

All these are due to incorrect perception. Once they are examined in proper conditions, their real nature is understood. The knowledge of oyster shell and silver, rope and snake or garland or stick and mirage and water is already existing in the perceiver. But because of the improper external conditions the perception is distorted. Likewise, the knowledge of our own real nature and unity with the Paramatman is already existing in the individual soul. The unreal nature of the visible phenomena is evident. But human beings fail to comprehend their own real nature and the unreality of the visible world. They think that the unreal is real and adore it because of the body, mind and intellect, which are seats of ajnanam. They create all the perversions. So once the cause, that is, ajnanam, is removed, jnanam will start shining. Of course, we need to know what ajnanam is and how to remove it.

In chapters 39 and 50 Hemadpant describes ajnanam and the ways to acquire jnanam by removing the ajnanam. Based on a conversation between Baba and the devotee Nana Chandorkar, Hemadpant explains what is ajnanam and how to get rid of it.

Once Nana was doing seva of Baba. While pressing Baba's feet, Nana was murmuring slokas from the fourth chapter of the Bhagavat Gita. When he reached the 34th verse, Baba asked him to explain the meaning of that particular verse:

Tadviddipranipatena, pariprashnena, sevaya

Upadekshyantitejnanam, jnaninastattvadarsinah

'Making prostrations at the guru's feet, giving one's life in the service of the guru and questioning the guru respectfully, then those who have attained the real knowledge will give instructions of that knowledge.' This is the meaning that Nana gave, which was according to what some great commentators had said. But Baba asked him to give the meaning word-by-word. Baba told him to use the word 'ajnanam' following the word 'te' instead of the word 'jnanam'. Baba said:

> Nana, take into consideration of the third metric foot, once again. Before the word 'jnanam' there is a sign of suspension. Bring that into the meaning.
>
> Chapter 39, verse 54

Jnanam is not a subject matter of words. It cannot be taught. So if the opposite word ajnanam is taken, it can

Ignorance

be discussed. Jnanam is to be realised by oneself. When ajnanam is removed, jnanam will be revealed. So the learned and wise will help the disciple recognise the ajnanam and the ways to remove it. Lord Shri Krishna also says in the Gita that jnanam is veiled by ajnanam, 'Just as the caul envelops the embryo or dust covers the mirror or ashes cover the embers, so does ignorance covers knowledge.'

Hemadpant says:

> The power of the inner vision of the eyes is jnanam. The veil or film over it which increases is Ajnanam and it is necessary to dispel it.
>
> Chapter 39, verse 59

> Just as the sun and the moon, even when they have an eclipse, are always shining and it is only our vision which has been obstructed by the coming in between by the planets Rahu and Ketu.
>
> Chapter 39, verse 62

> There is no obstruction to the sun and the moon. It is only our perception which is affected. Similarly, jnanam is unobstructed. It is self-evident and in its place.
>
> Chapter 39, verse 63

> Jnanam shines with its own lustre and is self-effected. It is like pure water covered with moss. The intelligent one, who removes this moss, will find the pure water.
>
> Chapter 39, verse 61

The pure consciousness which permeates the living and non-living objects of the visible universe is conditioned by time, space and forms. The inner pure consciousness residing inside the human body is conditioned by the body, mind and intellect. The pure consciousness that permeates the visible world is called God and its manifested counterpart is called Maya. Paramatman is the pure consciousness which is independent and exists apart from these two. It is formless, all pervading, omnipotent, omniscient and ever-existing. The visible universe is existing as a reflection in it. Even if the visible universe is destroyed, Paramatman will be there. Its nature is of omnipotent intelligence.

Realisation of these facts is pure knowledge. So the inner consciousness within the human body is the stable truth. When it is covered by a body, it is called jivatman. The consciousness of the visible universe is Atman (God). The pure consciousness, unrestrained by anybody or universe is Paramatman (Brahman). Thus jivatman, Atman and Paramatman all are, in essence, the same. Realising this fact is the real jnanam and incomprehension of it is ajnanam. A human being is unable to realise the jnanam because of the dense covering of the veil created by the body, mind and intellect. That is why Baba told Nana that the learned and wise will teach about ajnanam and when we are able to remove the veil of ajnanam, jnanam will shine by itself.

Types of Ajnanam

Hemadpant describes the types of ajnanam and the ways to dispel it:

> That the world is real is a great illusion. That is the dark veil over jnanam. This has to be dispelled first. Then only will Brahman manifest, which is the greatest jnanam.
>
> Chapter 39, verse 68

The visible world is an unreal one. It is formed by five elements and three properties and is perishable. What is permanent is the underlying pure consciousness. Human beings are stupefied by the splendid visible prakriti and believe that it is real and everlasting. By repeated thinking and believing, they give a concrete form to the outer universe. This is the principal type of ajnanam. Only devotion to God and sadguru can help in dispelling this. By devotion to God and sadguru, we get a sense of enquiry. This helps us to differentiate between the real and unreal and we will be able to distil the pure and real from the impure visible. Thus we will not be fearful about Maya anymore.

Next, Hemadpant says that enjoyment of sensual pleasures is the greatest ajnanam. He says that desire and anger are the greatest impediment in realising jnanam.

Whatever be the so-called pleasures of the five senses ultimately cause nothing but sorrow and are the greatest ajnanam.

Chapter 39, verse 89

Senses, intellect and mind are the abodes of these desires. With the help of these, the knowledge of the living being is dimmed and they are lured.

Chapter 50, verse 140

When there is obstruction to fulfilment of desire, then thwarted desire becomes anger. At every step it hinders liberation. This course of action is an impediment to knowledge.

Chapter 50, verse 134

Just as a clean mirror is covered by dust and the light of the fire by smoke, similarly knowledge that is controlled by anger and desires is covered by ignorance.

Chapter 50, verse 125

Desire and anger envelopes the foetus of knowledge like a membrane, just as the killer snake encircles the roots of the sandalwood tree.

Chapter 50, verse 138

Cravings and passions arise in the mind. Repeated thinking leads to action. Of the sensual pleasures, the most difficult to overcome are the temptations of the tongue and the genitals. Uncontrolled desires lead to sinful actions and moral downfall. If there are impediments in fulfilling our desires, it leads to anger. Anger manifests as heinous thoughts, rude and callous words and violent actions.

Hemadpant says that attachment to spouse, children, family, home and wealth is another type of ajnanam. The feeling of 'I' and 'mine' leads to emotional attachment to the family, children and wealth. We may toil day-and-night for the welfare of our spouse and children, thinking that all these transitory bodies are our own possessions. We may even indulge in abominable and corrupt means to support and fulfil their wishes. Even though we get repeated setbacks from these relatives, we are unable to break the chains of attachment. We fail to realise that our own body and all other visible things are transitory.

Pride arising out of knowledge and doubt are other types of ajnanam. Pride in our knowledge and learning is the most difficult type of ajnanam to remove. Excessive pride leads to arguments and conflicts. Pride in our own belief systems leads to contemptuous attitude towards other belief systems. It is because of this veil that people belonging to different religious beliefs fight with one another, leading to fanaticism.

Another type of ajnanam is doubt. Doubt occurs even in wise people. Doubts occur about the existence of Paramatman and mukti even in learned and wise people. Thus they deviate from the true path because of their own uncertainty and doubt.

How to Destroy Ajnanam

The body–mind–intellect conglomerate prevents us from realising our real, true nature and causes the cycle of births and deaths to continue. In this visible world nothing is permanent. The mind creates the world and its objects. The feeling of bondage is also created by the mind. We have to control our mind, get rid of all vices and impurities and direct it towards the path of devotion. We should see and worship the Paramatman as the all-pervading eternal essence and as the internal reality which resides in all living beings. Thus we will obtain the grace of God and the guru and achieve oneness with the Paramatman, that is, self-knowledge or jnanam.

When ajnanam is removed, jnanam will shine. Now let us see how to destroy the ajnanam. Hemadpant says:

> If you want to obtain sandalwood, then you will have to kill the snake coiled around it. Remove the veil of desire and anger and attain the store of knowledge.
>
> Chapter 50, verse 140

> The mind is tainted by ignorance. The mind cannot be cleansed without devotion to God and without devotion, knowledge is not born.
>
> Chapter 50, verse 115

> Therefore, know what is ignorance at the outset. After it is described and you derive the lesson therefrom, only then will the bondage be broken. Devotion is the only means to do that.
>
> Chapter 50, verse 116

> Knowledge itself means attainment of self-realisation, for which the main thing is to destroy ignorance. Unless devotion to God is achieved, the power of Maya is boundless.
>
> Chapter 50, verse 118

The Lord exists in all living beings. Doing a yagna for knowledge and other worship, if one sees Krishna (i.e., the Lord) as all-pervasive, ignorance burns away leaving behind knowledge.

Chapter 50, verse 120

Hemadpant explains that desires and anger are the greatest veils covering the true knowledge, self-knowledge. We must practise devotion to God to dispel the impurity of ignorance. We should comprehend that the same Lord is present in all fellow living beings. Along with devotion, we should continue the methods of worship and other prescribed actions. Then we will be able to attain the real knowledge, that is, the unity between jivatman and Paramatman.

This is symbolically described as a yagna (sacrifice). A yagna is conducted by ritualistically offering something to a higher godly entity to obtain precious blessings or boons. The chosen godly figure is propitiated by chanting specific mantras and pouring ghee or clarified butter and other offerings in a ritual fire. Occasionally, an animal like a goat or a horse is also sacrificed. It is believed that the animal thus offered attains salvation. The performer of the sacrifice obtains boons from the deity. Lord Rama's father King Dasaratha had performed a sacrifice to obtain children – putrakameshti yagna. Lord Rama and King Yudhishtara had performed rajasuya yagna.

Hemadpant describes an unusual type of yagna to obtain the real knowledge in verses 120–124 of chapter 50. The courtyard for the yagna is the five elements of the universe, the being is the one who performs the yagna, the axiom 'I am Brahman' is the pillar to which sacrificial animal is tied, the belief that there is a difference between a living being and God is the sacrificial animal. The only requirements for this yagna are the five senses and the five pranas. The being should kindle the fire of knowledge in the hollow space of his mind and intellect and offer ignorance as oblations in place of the ghee to make the fire burn brightly. Thus, by burning the difference between a living being and God, that is, by offering the veil of ajnanam, the knowledge about the unity of consciousness manifests. At the end of the sacrifice, the being is bathed in the water of purification, or in other words, he is completely engrossed in the bliss of self-knowledge.

Human beings should develop discriminative thinking and realize what is good for their progress and what is binding them in ignorance. Thus, they should be able to remove their ignorance completely.

Hemadpant says:

> Discrimination between transient and permanent objects destroys sin. That itself grants refinement and rectification and that itself creates knowledge.
>
> Chapter 50, verse 177

> But the discriminative thinking does not develop spontaneously in a being who is bound in conditioned existence. It is developed by keeping the company of holy and wise persons, or satsang, and listening to their upadesh, or teachings.

> Therefore, the remedy to do away with the harm or evil of ignorance is upadesh. The wise ones weary themselves by giving the upadesh of what constitutes ignorance.
>
> Chapter 50, verse 185

By resorting to satsang and studying the sacred scriptures, we receive dispassion and wisdom and thereby we become capable of discriminating between the real and unreal. Once we grasp what is real and what is unreal, that itself is jnanam. Most people think that their physical or the subtle body is the real self. They are ruled by passions and harmful feelings like jealousy, pride, lust, greed, anger, avarice, malice and so on. However much we may try to change their attitude, it seems impossible to do so. Such people have to undergo innumerable births and deaths. Swami Samartha Ramadas, in his holy text *Dasabodha*, says that we can carve any type of a sculpture out of a stone by hard work, but to change a human being's deep-rooted beliefs and attitudes is impossible. But if such people resort to the holy feet of a saint, they can escape from ruin. Association with saints and their teachings help to shed the body-mind-intellect conglomerate which is nothing but ajnanam or ignorance.

Conclusion

Ignorance is the greatest enemy of humankind because it obscures their self and pushes them into a cycle of repeated births and deaths. Belief in the reality of the visible and its adoration, attachment to the pleasures of the senses, body, family, wealth, status and fame, and destructive feelings like greed, enmity, avarice, malice, pride, doubt and so on, put fetters on human beings. The veil of the body–mind–intellect combination or ajnanam covers the light of pure knowledge. By developing devotion to God, performing satsang and taking upadesh from the holy people, we acquire the capacity to recognise the veil of ignorance and remove it. Thus when we become pure and free from desire and anger, we realise the unity of consciousness. Then the hidden jnanam manifests itself. We are unaffected by the visible, rejoice in the bliss of self-knowledge and are released from the cycle of births and deaths. This is also called liberation.

ATTACHMENT

The body, home, son, wife – 'I' and 'mine' – these are fruitless toils and turmoils of human life. All this is momentary Maya, like the noon shadow.
Chapter 27, verse 11

There is no person without attachment. It is not possible for such a being to exist. Some are attached to certain things and some others to something else. A human being is looking for attachment.
Chapter 10, verse 126

He who is not aware of means of happiness other than wealth, wife and children, for him Brahman is chimerical. It cannot attain peace for you.
Chapter 16, verse 30

3

ATTACHMENT

> For some the object of attachment is children; for some money, honour and riches; some are attached to the body, the house or popularity; some to attaining knowledge.
>
> Chapter 10, verse 127

Attachment means a strong feeling of being emotionally close to someone or something. Different people have different attachments. Some people are attached to wealth, position or status. Some people are attached to gaining knowledge. Most people are mainly attached to their wife or husband and children. They try hard to maintain their family. They think that their body, wife, children, house, wealth, relations, friends and so on are permanent and they spend their whole life maintaining them. The material world is their reality. Their attachment to their family and relations bring endless misery and anguish. Lord Dattatreya cites the example of a pigeon to show how individuals feel attached to their spouse and children and how it causes their self-destruction. Lord Dattatreya is the manifestation of the Trinity and is Jagad Guru, that is, a teacher to the whole world.

Once King Yadu met an ascetic who was very young and full of bliss, untouched by worldly concerns. The ascetic was Lord Dattatreya. King Yadu asked Lord Dattatreya how he could be so unconcerned, happy and blissful. Lord

Dattatreya answered that he learned the art of living from his 24 teachers. Then he listed the 24 teachers and the lessons he imbibed from them. These teachers were the elements and creatures of the universe like water, air, fire, reptiles, insects, human beings and so on. The self-learning which he acquired by observing them enabled him to live in the world without getting affected by it. One of the main lessons he learnt was to be free internally without attachment to anything perishable and to be always blissful by living in one's inner self. Of his teachers, the pigeon's state exemplifies a man who leads family life.

The Story of the Pigeon

A pigeon and his wife lived in a nest in a forest. They were deeply in love. The wife became pregnant and in due course laid some eggs. The eggs hatched and baby pigeons were born. The parents were very happy. They looked after their children very affectionately. One day while the parents had gone in search of food for their children, a hunter saw the baby pigeons and caught them in a net. When the mother pigeon saw that her helpless children caught in the net, she lamented loudly and frantically flew into the trap to rescue them, but got caught instead. When the father pigeon saw that his entire family been caught in the net, he could not tolerate their state and he also flew into the net. The happy hunter took all the birds and left.

This story is mentioned here to highlight the state of a family man – how he gets deeply attached to the family life. A husband or wife should definitely execute responsibilities to the family and should be loving and caring towards children and other members of the family. But at the same time, they should not nurture too much hope or anxiety about children or spouse or other relatives. Even while maintaining a family through righteous ways, people should not get into deep attachment and desire to possess the relations forever. The moral of this story is that even if a person is fully immersed in family life, he should be internally free from its turmoils.

In Satcharita Hemadpant says:

> Our existence in this world is of a duration no longer than a flash of lightning. How can people find moments of complete happiness when they are caught between the jaws of destiny?
>
> Chapter 14, verse 21

> Mother, father, sister, husband, wife, son, daughter, cousin – they are like logs of wood which float in the current of a river.
>
> Chapter 14, verse 22

> They seem to be together for a moment. Then they scatter by the movement of the wave and go separately, never to meet again.
>
> Chapter 14, verse 23

Hemadpant further says this material life is like a whirlpool:

> In the stormy waters of hope, there are whirlpools of son, wife and friends; crocodiles of passion, rage, etc.; and sharks in the form of various diseases.
>
> Chapter 17, verse 122

> At times there is a temporary aversion for hours together. There is a mental conflict, an eruption; but the bond cannot be broken.
>
> Chapter 17, verse 123

Because of ignorance, human beings think that their body is their real self and with the thought of 'I' and 'mine', the tree of material life sprouts. They get attached to their worldly ways and are bound by both meritorious and sinful actions and experiences the resultant pleasure and pain. Thus they are caught in the cycles of birth and death. The reason for a physical birth is the previous unfulfilled desires and latent tendencies.

Attachment is an obstacle to self-realisation. One is unable to avoid the cycles of birth and death. This fact was told by Baba to the greedy miser, the ascetic Vijayananda and the Ramadasi who could not part with even one of his religious texts.

The Greedy Miser

Once a greedy miser, who was deeply attached to wealth, property, cattle and family, wanted instant Brahmajnanam from Baba. He thought he lacked only in Brahmajnanam and he had heard that Baba was a liberal donor like Karna in Mahabharata, in imparting divine knowledge. But this wealthy man was not ready to give even five rupees to Baba, that too as a loan. And he wanted the most precious thing for humans – knowledge of Brahman. Only a person who is detached, dispassionate, compassionate and wise can think of acquiring self-knowledge. Baba communicated to the person that attachment to money, family and wealth is the primary obstacle in attaining self-realisation.

In the same manner, we can observe the fate of another teacher of Lord Dattatreya – a honey bee. A person engrossed in amassing wealth faces the same fate as a honeybee. A honeybee collects nectar from flowers and stores it in honeycombs. It does not use the honey itself, but simply keeps on storing it. If any creature accidentally comes near the honeycomb, the honey bee stings it. But human beings take away the honey. A greedy person amasses wealth and does not use the money nor donates it to charity. Later someone will take the wealth away or the person will die without realising the real purpose of life.

The Ascetic Vijayanand

The ascetic Vijayanand came for Baba's darshan while he was travelling to Manasa Sarovar. Later, while talking to Somadeva Swamiji, he learnt about the difficulties of the journey and decided to cancel the pilgrimage. He stayed in Shirdi. Meanwhile, he got a letter from his home stating that his mother was ailing. Depressed and anxious, he sought Baba's permission to go to his mother. The omniscient Baba knew that the ascetic's own end was near. So Baba told him that attachment is not befitting for an ascetic.

> If you were so fond of your mother, then why did you don this garb (of a Sanyasi)? Attachment does not befit these clothes. You have blemished this ochre garb.
>
> Chapter 31, verse 35

Baba advised him to do ritual reading of *Bhagavatapuranam* and concentrate his mind on God.

> Being desireless, hear that book or read it with concentration and contemplate on it night and day.
>
> Chapter 31, verse 47

Within a few days Vijayananda passed away. Thus Baba's words came to be true.

The Ramadasi and *Vishnusahasranama*

Once a Ramadasi stayed in Shirdi. He used to read *Adhyatma Ramayana* and *Vishnusahasranama* regularly. One day Baba wanted to give the *Vishnusahasranama* to Shama. So Baba sent the Ramadasi to the market saying that he needed senna pods as he was suffering from stomach pain. When the Ramadasi left for the market, Baba took the *Vishnusahasranama* and gave it to Shama. Baba told him about the greatness of the book and asked him to keep it

Attachment

reverentially and to read it regularly. When the Ramadasi came back, he saw what had happened and became very furious. He launched a strong verbal attack on Shama. He said if Shama did not return his book, he would dash his head in front of him and scatter his blood profusely. Then Baba spoke to the Ramadasi:

> Every day you read the *Adhyatma Ramayana* and recite the *Sahasranama*. Yet you have not discarded your passions which are uncontrolled. And you call yourself a Ramadasi?
>
> Chapter 27, verse 114

> What kind of a Ramadasi are you? You should be absolutely detached. But you are not able to overcome your intense desire to possess the book. What name can be given for this behaviour?
>
> Chapter 27, verse 115

> A true Ramadasi should have no attachment, but look at the young and old with equality. You are harbouring enmity for this boy and coming to blows for this book?
>
> Chapter 27, verse 116

A person who had given up everything worldly and was engaged in the reading and reciting of religious texts could not part with even a book nor keep an even mind. We can imagine the extent of attachment in a worldly person! We saw that the root cause of attachment is ignorance – ignorance about our own real nature. In this world, no one belongs to anyone. No one is meant to be there for anybody's happiness. All are prey to destiny, that is, death. Whatever happiness we think we get from our relations and friends is the result of our imagination. When false imagination is removed, ignorance will be destroyed. We must be able to do our duties according to the respective stations of life, but we should not involve in them with emotional attachment. When sage Vasishta was instructing Lord Shri Rama, he told him about the story of Choodala, the enlightened queen who led her husband Sikkidwaja to self-realisation. This queen became enlightened by self-enquiry and realised her real nature as pure consciousness. Unaffected by pain or pleasure, without any mental notions and ideas, she remained in supreme peace while leading a royal life. On the other hand, the king, who was deluded by his own mental notions, gave up his wife, kingdom and all royal pleasures. Then he went to the forest to lead an ascetic life. He thought that equanimity of mind and supreme peace could be gained only by such a life. But his attachment to the idea of renunciation itself became an obstacle in gaining enlightenment. Later, Choodala disguised herself as a Brahmin youth and made him realise what it was really which had to be renounced. She made him realise that he had to renounce his mind and ego and he should live with discrimination and dispassion. Instead of abandoning his prescribed duties, he should give up the mental attachment to those duties. By dissolving the mind into naught, we can achieve supreme peace. When there is no sorrow or pain, that state itself is supreme peace. That was what the king should have been seeking.

All relations and objects which we consider as our own do not really belong to us. In this world human beings are born because of their past deeds and experiences, that is, the fruits of their own actions. Each one of us is a lone traveller who is heading towards the final destination of death. But our mind conceives others, like our family, as belonging to us. So we get mentally bound to them and experience pain and pleasure with them. We completely forget about our real nature of pure consciousness. Ignorant thoughts, resultant passions and cravings and hurtful feelings bind us more and more to material life.

Attachment

In this context, Baba's advice to Kaka Mahajani's friend and his manager Dharamsi Theja Bhai is very relevant. Dharamsi was full of pride about his position and went with Kaka Mahajani on the condition that since Baba was a mere human being, he would not bow down to him or give him dakshina. But after meeting Baba, Dharamsi's pride and earlier resolutions disappeared. He became humble and clear of mental impurities. He bowed down at Baba's feet and without being asked, offered dakshina also. Baba gave him valuable instructions. Baba said:

> There was a fickle-minded man. He was prosperous. He was free from physical and mental afflictions. But he took on him needless anxieties.
>
> Chapter 35, verse 115

> He carried upon himself unnecessary burdens. He wandered hither-and-thither and had no peace of mind. Sometimes he dropped the burdens and other times carried them again. His mind knew no steadiness.
>
> Chapter 35, verse 116

Dharamasi had adequate wealth and respect but he was not contented. Without having the slightest reason, Dharamsi was always worried. He was burdened by severe imaginary problems and was always lost in them. His attachment to material objects, wealth and relations made him preoccupied with the thoughts related to them. This used to totally ruin his mental peace.

Baba again told him:

> Pull down the oil-monger's wall between us totally, so that the road is widened to enable us to meet each other.
>
> Chapter 35, verse 47

Baba wants his devotees to be free of attachment and subsequent pride and anxieties. By severing the ties with both attachment and misery, we should be even-minded and humble. Then only will we be able to achieve grace.

Conclusion

Attachment to family, wealth and worldly objects is an impediment to spiritual progress. It is the mind which creates attachment by producing ignorant thoughts. If the same mind is empty of thoughts, that itself is the state of liberation. If a person can live in a mindless state and dedicate all the actions as offerings to pure consciousness residing in the body, that person is a liberated soul. Then it does not matter whether he or she is a king or a queen or a family person, because they attained supreme peace not by renouncing any ordained external conditions but by controlling the mind and its desires. But this state of the mind does not occur unless wisdom is applied. Wisdom springs from discrimination (i.e., being able to know what is real and what is unreal) and dispassion. Discrimination and dispassion are achieved by association with saints and devotion to God. Desire for saintly association arises from pure, selfless deeds. Then, the external circumstances and objects themselves will act as a catalyst for spiritual progress –they will no longer bind one with the chains of attachment.

GREED

The greed for money is very difficult. It is a deep whirlpool of pain, full of crocodiles in the form of conceit and jealousy. Only a desireless person can swim across these difficult waters.
                                        Chapter 17, verse 68

There is unending enmity between avarice and Brahman. How can he attain salvation and practise self-denial who has no time for meditation?
                                        Chapter 17, verse 69

Where there is greed, there is no peace, no contentment, nor restfulness. All means (of achieving Brahman) turn to dust when avarice takes hold of the mind.
                                        Chapter 17, verse 70

Greed for money became an obstacle, and he was blinded by it despite having eyes. He totally forgot brotherly love and became ready to kill him.
                                        Chapter 46, verse 127

Money is a big snare! Even the affluent are troubled by it.
                                        Chapter 47, verse 150

4

GREED

Passion, anger and greed are the three doors to hell; and are the cause for the destruction of the self. Therefore they should be definitely discarded.

Chapter 14, verse 150

Greed is a major vice. Greed or avarice is a strong, selfish and excessive desire to continuously get more of something, especially money – more than what is needed. It is a type of a mental craving to amass material goods or wealth. It stems from the deep-rooted ignorant thinking of 'I' and 'mine'. Greedy persons think that their body and possessions are real. Even though they see numerous humans take birth into this world alone and die alone, leaving everything behind, they are unable to realise the impermanency of the physical world. Even when their own relatives die in front of them, they do not have the wisdom to think properly. Instead, they continue to grab as many possessions as they can. Such avarice is the densest delusion that exists in the human mind.

A greedy person lives with a deep-rooted body consciousness. The human body is made up of the gross body, which is the frame and the subtle body, which is the active and causal body which is constituted by the three qualities. Gross body is called the physical sheath. Subtle body consists of a vital sheath, mental sheath and intellectual sheath. Causal is called the blissful sheath.

The subtle body, physical body and the causal body get enlivened by the self or the consciousness, which is a part of the Paramatman. When body, mind and intellect are pure, we can find peace and happiness in our own self. But this is not possible for most people, especially for greedy persons. A greedy person's mind is deluded by excessive desires and that, in turn, leads to other harmful tendencies like anger, miserliness, jealousy, pride, enmity and so on. Hemadpant says that passion, anger and greed are the most inauspicious traits and they are a hindrance in progressing on the path of spirituality.

By instructing a greedy miser, Baba conveys the message that a spiritual aspirant should submit his mind, intellect, ego, the five senses of action and perception and five pranas to the higher self and be desireless. This wealthy man had everything in plenty. He thought that the only thing he lacked in life was Brahmajnanam. So he went to Shirdi for Baba's darshan. He hired a tonga for the to-and-fro journey. He requested Baba for imparting Brahmajnanam. Baba told him:

> Many people ask for wealth; or ask for cures for ailments; or ask for power and honour; and, always happiness.
>
> Chapter 16, verse 40

> People come running to Shirdi only for the sake of temporal happiness and become the followers of a fakir like me. Nobody asks for Brahman ever.
>
> Chapter 16, verse 41

> Such people (seeking worldly benefits) are in plenty. But I experience a drought where people like you are concerned. I long for those seeking Brahman. This seems to be an opportune time for me.
>
> Chapter 16, verse 42

Baba gave a short discourse on the greatness of Brahman. Baba then called a young boy and told him to go to Nandu's house and ask for a loan of five rupees. The boy soon came back and said that Nandu's house was locked from outside. Baba sent the boy to Bala and a few other people for the loan. But the boy could not find anyone of them. The omniscient Baba knew that Nandu, Bala and others would not be at home. He also knew that the wealthy man had 250 rupees in his pocket. The loan which Baba wanted was very small and that too for a short while. Yet the wealthy man did not offer to give it to Baba though he was asking for the priceless knowledge of Brahman! Any simple, straightforward person who had genuine love for Baba would not have silently watched this attempt to borrow money. The wealthy man neither gave the money, nor was ready to sit patiently. He had engaged the tonga for the return journey and hence he was in a hurry to go back. So he told Baba, 'Baba, show me Brahman quickly.' Baba replied:

> To show you Brahman where you are sitting, I have tried certain means so far. Did you not follow anything?
>
> Chapter 16, verse 72

> You have been watching us while sitting here. You possess 50 times more money (than five rupees) in your pocket. Take it out now. Let us see. Confusion is in your pocket.
>
> Chapter 17, verse 63

The gentleman put his hand in his pocket and took out a packet which consisted of 25 notes of 10 rupees each, and counted them. He was ashamed in his heart and thought to himself, 'How well Maharaj knows the inner secrets!' He put his head on Baba's feet and anxiously asked for his blessings.

At that time Baba said:

Greed

> Now wrap up your fake Brahman. Till your greed is not destroyed, you will never realise Brahman. He whose mind is attached to his family and possessions (sons, farm, animals, etc.), how can he achieve Brahman, till constant awareness of his wealth is not abandoned?
>
> Chapter 17, verses 66, 67

Baba wants his devotees to have a dispassionate attitude towards life and live happily while performing all the necessary duties. The devotees should be desireless and always aware of their real goal. Greed not only hinders our spiritual progress, but also makes us an object of contempt. Because of greed, good human qualities will desert us. Greed breeds anger, enmity, callousness, cruelty and doubt. It will even block other people's spiritual aspiration as well.

In this context, see what was Parasurama's experience. Parasurama conquered all kings by defeating them 21 times. Then he took their possessions and lands and donated them all to Brahmins. After that, Parasurama did not have any place to conduct his austerities, as he had donated everything to the Brahmins. He requested the ocean for some land. The ocean acceded and withdrew some of its water. Parasurama settled there and started his austerities. The Brahmins came to him and told him, 'You had donated all the lands to us. Therefore we are the custodians of all lands. So this land also belongs to us. Hence please move away from here.' Parasurama thought to himself, 'Wherever I go, these greedy Brahmins' will follow me and grab whatever I have.' Thinking thus, Parasurama entered into the ocean and sitting on the seabed, started to do his austerities! Such is the extent of greed, that it even forgets its benefactor.

An example of how greed hinders our desire for God realisation is given in Satcharita.

Story of Ramadasi Devotees

Once a group of devotees from Madras, who followed Ramadasi tradition and used to sing bhajans, came to Shirdi. They were on pilgrimage to many places. They had heard that Baba gave large sums to devotees, pilgrims, artists, beggars and so on. So to get some money, they came to Baba and started to sing devotional songs. The songs were only sung out of greed, not out of devotion. Only the wife of the leader had some devotion, others including the leader, his daughter and his sister-in-law did not. One day while they were taking Baba's darshan, Baba gave the darshan as Lord Rama to the leader's wife. Others, who were in the masjid at that time, saw only Baba's form. That lady had achieved a lot of spiritual progress earlier. When her mind was calm and relaxed, she used to get Lord Shri Rama's darshan. But when greed for money arose in her mind, the visions stopped. Now Baba reminded her about her earlier spiritual progress by giving her darshan as Lord Rama. The same night Baba also appeared in her husband's dream. The dream vision and the conversation he had with Baba in that dream, totally changed his attitude. Faith and devotion developed in him and then in all of the group. They received Baba's blessings. By Baba's grace, they could comfortably complete their pilgrimage and visited many more places than they had intended. The greed for money, which had occupied their mind earlier, totally vanished and they remembered Baba's mercy and grace for the rest of their lives.

Greed breeds anger and enmity. This pollutes our consciousness and imprisons us into rebirths of lower order. Once Baba described the story of the previous lives of two goats. They were brothers and killed each other because of greed and enmity. Baba also told about the story of the previous lives of a snake and a frog. Where there is greed, what can be expected? There is no thought about God, righteousness and morality.

Greed

In order to teach His devotees not to succumb to greed, Baba used to ask dakshina from them.

Baba and Dakshina

What was the meaning of dakshina and why did Baba ask dakshina?

To live in this world, money is necessary. The desirable path is to earn money through virtuous ways and use it for the maintenance of our family and for righteous deeds. To use money for worldly pleasures or amass it should never be our aim. By practising desirelessness and dispassion, we will be able to lead a family life and at the same time pursue the real purpose of human life. To imprint this fact on people's minds, Baba asked dakshina from them. Sometimes by repeatedly asking dakshina from the same person, he used to make even the wealthiest into a humble person. Both virtuous and non-virtuous people would throng to a saintly person. When Baba demanded dakshina, insincere aspirants would turn away.

Hemadpant explains the meaning of dakshina as follows:

Prajapathi's three progeny, viz., gods, demons and human beings, at the time of the completion of Brahmacharya, asked for upadesh. At that time, he uttered the alphabet 'da' as upadesh. What was the meaning of it? He asked them to check their interpretation. The gods understood it as 'danta' or to have restraint; the demons understood it as 'daya' or to be kind; the humans understood it as 'dana' or to be charitable.

Dakshina is a type of donation which is given at the time of worship of a deity as well as worship of a saint, guru or sage. Dakshina should be given with reverence and faith. Hemadpant says:

Baba also, as per this letter 'da' asked the same thing from his devotees for their own good – be kind, be charitable, be restrained. You will get great happiness.

Chapter 14, verse 146

Greed is man's major vice. Even then, to save man from the deep, dark pits of greed, Sainath, the ocean of kindness, stretches his arm and pulls them out.

Chapter 14, verse 142

Baba never allowed his devotees to be caught in the web of greed for money. Baba's treasure of Brahmajnanam will be available to only those pure devotees who are not tempted by money. Those devotees who have earnest yearning for spiritual realisation follow Baba's advice and reach their goals. Only a person who is not greedy for material wealth can completely surrender his whole self for spiritual achievement. For ordinary, worldly people, Baba gave this lesson by demanding dakshina. But for those aspirants who had a higher stature, Baba expected complete detachment from greed. In contrast to the wealthy miser, there were many selfless devotees who were not tempted by money and submitted their life and material wealth at Baba's feet. Baba's famous devotees like Mhalasapathy, Kaka Dikshit and the millionaire Buti were all selfless and had never harboured greed for wealth. So they could progress spiritually. On the other hand, Bade Miyan, who had the rare fortune of receiving Baba's favour and proximity, could not progress spiritually because of his greed and hankering for respect.

Mhalasapathy, the Selfless Devotee

Mhalasapathy was the first person who greeted Baba as 'Sai'. Since then he served Baba selflessly. He was the priest of the Khandoba temple. He used to stay in the masjid in the night, but never slept. Once Baba went into samadhi for three days after entrusting his physical body to him. Mhalasapathy kept Baba's body on his lap for three full days, not heeding to people's suggestions and instructions to bury him, because they thought Baba had left his body.

Mhalasapathy was very poor. Once, seeing his condition, one devotee offered him a box full of silver coins. But he said he could not accept it unless Baba agreed. Baba asked him whether he or the money was more valuable. Mhalasapathy answered that Baba was valuable to him and did not accept the money. He was pure of heart, selfless and devoted to Baba and surrendered to him completely. So Baba graced him and thus he became an advanced spiritual soul. Otherwise how could he keep the physical body of Baba, the incarnation of Paramatman on his lap?

Kaka Dikshit

Hari Sitaram Dikshit was a famous solicitor from Mumbai. He had Western education and was wealthy. Kaka had a fall while boarding a train in London. No treatment was of any benefit and subsequently he became lame. His friend Nana Chandorkar advised him to have Baba's darshan to be relieved of his lameness. Dikshit went for Baba's darshan and, instead, prayed for removing the lameness of his mind. He surrendered to Baba wholeheartedly, gave up his job, and built a wada in Shirdi for devotees. Kaka's wada was convenient for the devotees who came to Shirdi for Baba's darshan. Because of his generosity, devotees were benefitted. In contrast to the wealthy man's miserliness and greed, Kaka's generosity is laudable. Baba took care of his entire being and at the end he had a peaceful death.

Buti, the Selfless Millionaire

Buti was a pious and virtuous devotee. He was a millionaire. He used to visit Shirdi frequently for Baba's darshan. He thought of building a home in Shirdi and staying there permanently so that he could have Baba's darshan every day. One day Baba appeared in his dream and asked him to build a wada. Buti sought Baba's permission for building a wada with a temple of Muralidhar or Lord Krishna. Baba gave his permission. While the wada was being built, Baba became ill and before he attained Mahasamadhi, he asked to be taken to Buti's Wada. That wada is the present Samadhi mandir where millions of devotees from all over the world throng to have Baba's darshan. Sai devotees will always remember Buti gratefully for his generosity. Buti's life highlights the fact that Sai devotees should be selfless and they should avoid greed for hoarding money. Baba always preached that money should be used for virtuous purposes and for the benefit of the humanity, not hoard it greedily or spend it for trivial pleasures.

Bade Miyan
Baba would distribute all the money he received as dakshina from the devotees. Bade Miyan was getting ₹50 every day. He also was given a special place near Baba in the masjid at the time of lunch, after the aarati. Once on the day of Deepavali festival, he felt offended for some reason and did not come for lunch. Baba waited to eat till Bade Miyan was located and brought to the masjid. But Bade Miyan was unable to rise above greed and selfishness. So he could not progress spiritually. He remained lost in the mesh of money, food and worldly desires.

Conclusion
Greed is a vicious feeling. It hinders the natural evolution of the human soul. It results in anger and enmity. Devotees should avoid greed as well as excessive and unrighteous desires. Practising dispassion and being charitable purifies the mind. A purified mind is a fertile land for the seed of devotion to grow and receive the grace of the guru and God.

ENMITY

Mutual enmity causes one to fall from a higher state of life to a lower. Natural evolution of life is destroyed by debt, animosity and murder.

Chapter 47, verse 32

Both were wicked and deeds of both of them have been dreadful. The sins of their past lives have been terrible, and they have been born in another form of existence, to suffer the fruit of their actions.

Chapter 47, verse 54

On account of the enmity in the previous birth, Veerabhadrappa was born as a snake and pursued Channabasappa, the frog. In the end Veerabhadrappa caught him.

Chapter 47, verse 190

Though they were real brothers, they had great greed for money, which brought enmity between them, because of their own deeds and fate coming together, which brought immense suffering.

Chapter 46, verse 124

ENMITY

> These, that you see as goats, were brothers in their past lives. Their end came because of their in-fighting. This brought such a result.
>
> Chapter 46, verse 122

Enmity is a state of feeling of active opposition or hostility. Enmity is a by-product of mental impurities like lust, anger, greed, pride, infatuation, jealousy and so on. We can observe this in Puranas as well as in present age. In Mahabharata, Kauravas' greed for kingdom and riches resulted in their enmity towards Pandavas. Thus the Kurukshetra war was fought for the kingdom. The king of Chedi, Sisupala, was jealous of Shri Krishna and harboured extreme enmity towards the Lord. In Ramayana, Surupanakha was infatuated with Rama and Lakshmana and eventually Lakshmana maimed her. Surupanakha reported her plight to her brother Ravana and this led to his enmity with Rama. Even in the present times, these facts are very relevant. Some people become jealous of another person's riches and success and become inimical towards him and try to defame him. A person's angry words and behaviour will create enmity and ill-feeling in other people. If a person harbours desire to possess another person's assets, it creates enmity and undesirable acts. Baba always preached peace, mutual harmony, love and forgiveness. These qualities are beneficial for a spiritual aspirant as well as a general person. Baba said that enmity destroys the natural evolution and causes a person to fall from a higher state to a lower one.

In Satcharita, Hemadpant mentions two stories which describe the ill-effects of enmity.

The Story of Two Goats

Once Baba was returning from Lendi to the masjid along with some devotees. He saw a herdsman with a flock of goats. He felt sudden love and compassion for two of the goats. He purchased them by paying Rs.32 to the owner. Bringing them near him, Baba lovingly caressed them. The correct price of each of the two goats was at most four rupees. But Baba had given Rs.16 each. Tatya and Shama scoffed at Baba's behaviour. They asked Baba why he overpaid. Baba asked them to buy some lentils, feed the goats and then return them to the owner. Baba's command was obeyed. Thus the money spent on the goats went waste.

Then Baba told Tatya and Shama about the unusual story of the goats' past life. The goats were brothers in their previous birth. At first there was a lot of love and affection between them. But both of them had greed for money. The older brother was lazy. The younger brother was industrious, so he could accumulate wealth. The elder brother, because of greed, nursed wicked thoughts of killing the younger brother. Enmity developed between them. They came to know each other's negative thoughts. One day they fought like enemies. One of them grievously injured the other's head with a big stick. The other, with the help of an axe, likewise hit his brother. After a while both died. To undergo the effects of their past actions, they were reborn as goats. When Baba saw them, he felt compassion for them. Baba wanted to give them refuge. But because of their heinous past actions, this was hindered by the intervention of Tatya and Shama. So Baba returned them to the herdsman.

The Story of the Snake and the Frog

One day, in the morning, Baba set out for a walk. He reached a river bank and sat down. A wayfarer came and bowed at his feet. The wayfarer requested Baba to visit his house. At that time a frog began to croak loudly and piteously. The wayfarer asked who was crying. Baba replied that a frog had got into great difficulty because of its past actions. He said:

> We have to reap what we sow in our past life. One should endure one's destiny calmly. There is no use crying about it.
>
> Chapter 47, verse 50

The wayfarer went to confirm what Baba had said and he saw that a deadly snake was about to swallow a huge frog. He reported this to Baba. Baba replied that he had travelled so far to save the frog and he would not allow it to die. He went to the scene and addressed the snake as Veerabhadrappa and commanded him to release Channabasappa, the frog. He told them to give up enmity and remain at peace. No sooner than the words were uttered, the snake left the frog, quickly entered the deep waters of the river and disappeared. The frog also went and hid in the thick bushes.

Then Baba told the story of the past two lives of the snake and the frog.

Veerabhadrappa was a rich miser in his earlier life. He cheated the people who entrusted him the task of renovation of an old Siva temple. Because of greed, he misappropriated his wife's jewellery which was offered to the Lord and also cheated a destitute woman called Dubaki, who had mortgaged her land to him. After sometimes, it rained heavily and there was a frightful storm. Lightning struck that place and the three of them died. The rich man was then reborn in Mathura in a poor Brahmin family and

Enmity

was named Veerabhadrappa. His wife was reborn as Gauri, the temple priest's daughter. Dubaki was reborn as a male called, Channabasappa in Gurava caste, who worshipped Lord Siva.

The poor Brahmin Veerabhadrappa left his home in search of fortune and reached the priest's house. The priest liked him and thought of getting his daughter Gauri married to him. With Baba's blessings, the priest conducted his daughter's marriage with Veerabhadrappa. As years went by, Veerabhadrappa became more greedy for money. He went to Baba and told him about his wants. Baba assured him that the time for good fortune was very near.

That year, the price of the barren land shot up. A purchaser bought the land for one lakh rupees. He paid half the amount in cash and agreed to pay the other half in instalments to Gauri. He would pay the remaining half within twenty-five years – every year he would pay two thousand rupees with interest. Channabasappa claimed half of the interest as his share because he said that the land belonged to Lord Siva and the Gurav had the first claim on whatever money was offered to the Lord. But Veerabhadrappa did not agree to give anything to him. Baba advised them that Gauri was the sole heiress of the money and they should act according to her wishes. Veerabhadrappa became angry on hearing this. He abused Baba, went home and shouted at Gauri. Gauri had a vision in which Lord Siva instructed her to keep the money with her, heed to Channabasappa's advice regarding temple expenses and to consult Baba for any guidance. She informed this to Baba. Baba advised her to keep the capital with her and to give half of the interest earned to Channabasappa.

At that time, Veerabhadrappa and Channabasappa came there quarrelling. When Baba explained about Gauri's vision, Veerabhadrappa became insane with fury. He started threatening Channabasappa that he would kill him. Channabasappa was frightened and sought protection at Baba's feet. Baba assured him that he would not let him die at Veerabhadrappa's hands. Later Veerabhadrappa had a seizure and died. Channabasappa suffered from fears and apprehensions and died because of that. On account of the enmity in the previous birth, Veerabhadrappa was born as a snake and pursued Channabasappa, the frog. Remembering the assurance given in the previous life, Baba freed Channabasappa from the mouth of the snake.

What a pitiable state! This is the result of mutual enmity. Human body is superior to any other life forms. The only goal of human life is to reach God. From these two stories it is evident that hatred, enmity, malice and other negative feelings hinder the natural evolution of human life and they make it impossible to achieve self-realisation.

In this context here is a narration about psychological basis of enmity.

How Does the Feeling of Enmity Arise?

Our life revolves around attraction (raaga) and repulsion (dvesha). Based on these two mental states, we do actions which bring pleasure or pain. Human beings are made of gross, subtle and causal bodies. Pure consciousness enlivens all these components. Gross body is made of a combination of five elementary substances. The subtle body is made of subtle particles of the elemental substances without any combination. The ego, intellect, mind and mind-substance (passive mind) constitute the inner instrument, which is a part of the subtle body. The causal body is of the nature of primal energy. The three qualities (gunas) in their seed form, that is, prakriti, reside within the causal body. As prakriti unfolds in the human being, a dominant guna is carried forward depending on the deeds in the past life (karma). The gunas or qualities are sattva (purity), rajas (passion) and tamas (ignorance). The effect of these qualities is manifested as subtle and gross bodies. The quality of sattva is clarity, supreme calmness, contentment, joy, realisation of our own self and fixity in the Supreme-Self. Desire, anger, greed, ostentation, envy, egoism, jealousy, malice and so on are the bad qualities born of rajas. Ignorance, laziness, dullness, sleep, carelessness and delusion are qualities of tamas.

In association with the soul, the causal body sprouts into the subtle body in which ego, intellect, mind-substance and mind develop. Then, surrounding the subtle body, the gross body develops. Ego creates the 'I' and 'mine' feelings. Intellect is the discriminating faculty and the mind is the thinking faculty. Physical body is the vehicle for executing the actions, in demand of the subtle body. The subtle body is the manifest form of the causal body. If the predominant quality is passion, the feeling of 'I' and 'mine' will be very deep-rooted and the mind will be full of cravings and wicked desires. The intellect, which is the discriminating faculty, gets overpowered by ego. Such persons will be involved in activities which satisfies their ego and desires. The qualities of passion increase sensual desires, greed, anger, contentiousness and repulsiveness. They nourish hatred, animosity and increase arguments. Such persons become inimical to the people they perceive as a hindrance to fulfilling their desires. They argue and oppose those who have views, beliefs and opinions which are contradictory to their own. Continuous dwelling on negative thoughts of hatred, animosity and sensual pleasures leads to the quality of tamas (ignorance), confusion and delusion. Repeated thinking results in undesirable external actions.

Thus the qualities of passion and ignorance result in abominable actions like violence, oppression and even murder. When such persons commit harmful actions repeatedly, it leaves that kind of impression and patterns in the passive mind. When the physical body dies, the causal body and subtle impressions detach from the frame.

They carry the soul with them, receive another physical body and perpetuate the same quality and desires. Thus the soul (pure consciousness) remains veiled during repeated incarnations in physical bodies which are filled with passion and ignorance. If at the time of death, the quality of purity (sattva) predominates we will not have rebirths. If at the time of death, the quality of passion (rajas) predominates, we may reincarnate in a human body. But because of our actions we suffer pain and some pleasures and die in that state or at a still lower level. If at the time of death, the quality of ignorance (tamas) predominates, we will straightaway incarnate in a lower species. Thus it becomes very difficult for that soul to attain liberation. That is why Baba advised his devotees to refrain from enmity. Baba told that natural evolution of life is destroyed by debt, animosity and murder. Unpaid debt causes strained interactions, hatred and animosity. Intense enmity may impel a person to commit even murder.

People should refrain from enmity at either individual or group level. Conflict and enmity between different religious groups create unrest and fear in society. It hinders material growth and spiritual progress. Baba always advised Hindus and Muslims to live in harmony. Baba said:

> Ram and Rahim are one. There is not even the slightest difference. In that case why should there be an obstruction to devotion and indifferent behaviour towards each other?
>
> Chapter 10, verse 50

> Oh, you ignorant children, bring Hindus and Muslims together. Be firm on your path and have good thoughts. Then only, you will be able to go across to the other shore.
>
> Chapter 10, verse 51

Enmity

It is not good to argue; do not try to compete with each other. Always think of one's own (permanent) good and God will protect you.

Chapter 10, verse 52

If anyone harms you in anyway, you should not retaliate. If possible, try to oblige others.

Chapter 10, verse 54

Conclusion

Negative feelings such as enmity, hatred and malice should be avoided because they hinder our spiritual progress. We should not identify ourselves with actions based on passions, ignorance and delusion. Instead, we should nurture good thoughts and love all. We should be devoted to God and guru. This will help to purify the negative qualities. Otherwise, there will be a downfall in all aspects, including birth in lower forms.

SENSE CONTROL

A human being who does not know anything more than eating, sleeping, fear and sex is no better than an animal shorn of tail and horns.

Chapter 14, verse 19

One who panders to his senses can never hope to achieve spiritual progress. He who has a tight control over the senses alone can succeed.

Chapter 24, verse 43

The shrutis proclaim 'yadapanchavatishthante', that is, when all the five senses and intellect become steady, it is considered the highest state of yoga.

Chapter 24, verse 44

When the sense organs turn away from worldly pleasure and introverted, bliss of self is experienced and everything else will mean unhappiness.

Chapter 17, verse 98

6

SENSE CONTROL

If the sense organs begin to enjoy the objects of the senses, it will be a waste of energy and there is a fear of degradation at every step.

Chapter 39, verse 88

The importance of subduing the desires for sensual pleasures is repeatedly stressed in Satcharita. Uncontrolled enjoyment of sensual pleasures is harmful to the physical body and is an impediment to self-realisation. Compared to other living forms, human beings are superior because they are endowed with intelligence. Sensual pleasures and feelings are same for human beings and other creatures. With the help of intelligence, human beings should try to find out their real nature and realise oneness with the Paramatman. If we become a slave to sensual pleasures like animals, we will be using our body as an entrance to hell.

Human body is made up of five elements, it has five pranas, five sense-organs of perception and five sense-organs of action. When the sense-organs of perception come into contact with objects, human beings experience pain or pleasure, depending upon how painful or pleasing are their effects. Words are heard through ears and if they contain praise, the mind experiences it as pleasure; if the words contain criticism the mind experiences it as pain. Eyes see forms and if they are beautiful, the mind feels pleasure and happiness; if they are ugly, the mind feels dislike. If the forms are fearsome, the mind feels fear and pain. Good taste causes liking and bad taste creates dislike and trouble. Good smell causes pleasure through the nose, bad smell causes displeasure. Softness and hardness are qualities of touch; soft touch creates pleasure and hard touch such as a constricting embrace causes pain. So, depending on the type of sensation created by external objects, the mind decides whether it is pleasure or pain. Pleasure makes the mind content and satisfied. When the mind feels satisfaction, the desire which had arisen earlier gets fulfilled. This creates a memory and when the mind remembers and thinks about the pleasure, the desire arises again. When the desire arises, the mind directs the organs of action (voice, arms, legs, genitals and anus) to seek that object again. If it is fulfilled, the mind becomes satisfied again. This action gets repeated and it becomes vasana. This persists in the mental realm and the person becomes a slave to that pleasure.

Hemadpant says that both animals and human beings experience sense-pleasure in equal measure. Since this sense-pleasure is a state of mind, it has no distinction between learned and illiterate, poor and rich, male and female. The happiness which a king experiences by eating tasty food is as same as what a beggar experiences by eating some stale bread. Hemadpant says that the pleasure Lord Indra experiences in his celestial garden and which a donkey experiences in a heap of garbage is equal. Happiness derived from objects is merely a state of the mind.

What Is the Value of Sensual Pleasures?
The happiness derived from sense-objects is not real happiness. All sense-pleasures ultimately lead to sorrow. In chapter 39, Hemadpant describes how animals suffer by enjoying pleasure from just one sense organ.

Beguiled by sound, the deer ultimately meets its death. The elephant gets caught by its need for touch and has to bear the prick of the goad.

Chapter 39, verse 90

Entranced by the beauty of the light, the moth loses its life by burning its body; the fish which savours its food and bites the bait immediately loses its life.

Chapter 39, verse 91

The bee, bewitched by the fragrance, becomes a prisoner in the lotus. If involvement of just one sense causes so much harm, how fierce would the battle be when all five are involved?

Chapter 39, verse 92

This is the case of the animals on the land, creatures residing in water and the birds. Look at their bad condition. Even the knowledgeable run after sense pleasures. What else is it but ajnanam?

Chapter 39, verse 93

Human beings are intelligent, unlike the animals. But if they direct their intelligence and mind towards sensual pleasures, it will be injurious to their physical body. Excessive indulgence in sensual pleasures result in illness and moral downfall. It becomes a hindrance to spiritual progress also. Of the sense organs, the temptations of the tongue and the genital organs are the most difficult to overcome.

In *Gurucharitra*, there is a story describing how Lord Brahma created the world again, after a deluge, as per Lord Vishnu's command. During the creation process, Lord Brahma created four yugas (aeons) and sent the spirits of respective yugas to earth for spreading their influence.

These yugas are Kritayuga, Tretayuga, Dwaparayuga and Kaliyuga. Each yuga had been assigned a stipulated time period also. When it was the turn for Kaliyuga, Lord Brahma called the Kalipurusha – the spirit of the Kaliyuga. The characteristics of Kalipurusha are:

> Kalipurusha is ignorant and worldly. He has the face of the devil and he is always looking downwards. He is impure and he likes to fight with everyone at every step and for everything. He is cruel and has no compassion. He is an expert in fighting, hatred and revenge. He holds his penis firmly in his left hand and his tongue in his right hand. He dances in a terrible manner with excitement and sings filthy songs which are unbearable to hear. He rejoices in the company of cruel and evil persons.

Lord Brahma looked at the devil-like Kalipurusha and asked:

> Kalipurusha, why are you holding your tongue and your penis firmly in your hands?

Kalipurusha replied:

> Lord, with these two forces, I am going to conquer everyone in this world. This is my promise. This is my nature. My penis and my tongue are the secrets of my victory. Therefore I am holding them tightly in my hands.

True to Kalipurusha's words, a majority of human population is under the influence of these two forces. But Kalipurusha assured Lord Brahma that those who were devotees of God and saints, people who serve their guru and engage in righteous deeds, will not be influenced by these forces.

That happiness comes from sensual pleasures is really

false imagination. *Tripurarahasya* is the holy text which describes Lord Dattatreya's instructions to Parasurama. The Lord narrated a story to describe the importance of the association with the wise.

There lived a handsome prince Hemachuda and his beautiful and saintly wife Hemalekha. When the prince noticed that his newly wed wife was not interested in royal pleasures, he asked her about the reason for her disinterest. She replied that she was always engrossed in investigating what was the most lovable object and what was not so, and that she was not able to decide. The prince said that whatever gave pleasure was lovable and whatever gave pain was not. Hemalekha told the prince:

> Even the same thing, depending upon time, place and form, gives pleasure and pain alternately. Fire gives pleasure in winter, but pain in summer; it gives pleasure in a cool place and pain in a hot place. Depending upon whether it is less or more in quantum, the same things give different experiences. This fact is applicable to all kinds of pleasure – coolness, wealth, women, sons, kingdom and so on. Of all the objects of pleasure, a woman is considered the greatest. Likewise, males appear as attractive and lovely to women. In the case of union of man and woman, they will experience fatigue at the end of the rapturous excitement. There is the fatigue, as that of the bull carrying a burden. How do you deem that as happiness? Whatever happiness is caused to one by the excitement of nerves, while on the lap of the beloved, do not the dogs also have the same? The body is an aggregate of bones, flesh, blood, urine and so on. If people can find happiness in this disgusting assemblage, how are they different from worms? Oh, prince, this body of mine is supremely lovable to you. Mentally

separate the flesh and other parts. Are they still lovable? Extend this logic to the pleasures of eating, etc. What is eaten as delicious gets transformed as a filthy substance and this is the experience of all. Such being the nature of worldly objects, please tell me what is lovable and what is not?

From Hemalekha's reply we can understand the nature of sense-pleasures. The prince pondered over this matter and dispassion developed within him. He became able to seek the goal of human life.

Most people do not have the wisdom that Hemalekha had to analyse whether sensual pleasures are desirable or not. We need to nurture devotion and associate with saints and wise people. Thus we can get wisdom and detachment. Hemadpant describes one of his own experiences and also another devotee's experience and Baba's advice on those occasions.

Hemadpant and Grams

Once Hemadpant was doing Baba's service in the masjid. Shama noticed some grams in the folds of his coat and asked him about them. Hemadpant stretched his arm and the grams rolled down. People sitting there collected the fallen grams. Baba said that Hemadpant had a habit of eating alone and that it was the market day and Hemadpant had come with the grams in his hands. Hemadpant denied and said that till that day he had not seen the Shirdi market and that he never ate anything without sharing it with someone else. Baba replied:

> You share the food with whosoever is near you. But what do you do when you are alone? What can I also do? Do you remember me?

By making grams appear and through this conversation Baba advised Hemadpant as follows:

Sense Control

> Before the mind, intellect and other senses enjoy their objects, remember me first so that they become an offering to me slowly.
>
> *Chapter 24, verse 46*

> The senses can never remain without their objects; but if these objects are first offered to the guru, the attachment for them will naturally vanish.
>
> *Chapter 24, verse 47*

> If you desire anything, desire me only. If you are angry vent your anger on me only. Offer me your pride and obstinacy. Be devoted only to me.
>
> *Chapter 24, verse 48*

> Whenever desire, anger, and pride arise strongly, make me the object towards which to direct them.
>
> *Chapter 24, verse 49*

So when devotees think of Baba and offer all enjoyments to him, they will be able to decide whether they are desirable or not. Believing that Baba is always near us, we can easily shun undesirable objects and experiences.

> Let your intellect meditate on the guru, who is God; let your ears hear his stories; let your mind concentrate on him and let your tongue chant his name.
>
> *Chapter 39, verse 95*

> Let your feet take you to the abode of the guru; let your nose inhale fragrance of the flowers that have been offered to him; let your hands touch his feet in obeisance and let your eyes take his darshan.
>
> *Chapter 39, verse 96*

In this manner when employing all the senses for the Lord with love, the state of those devotees is blissful. What else is devotion to God?

Chapter 39, verse 97

Hemadpant says that when all the five senses and intellect become steady, it is considered as the highest yoga.

Nana Chandorkar's Experience

In chapter 49 Hemadpant describes Nana Chandorkar's experience. Once when Chandorkar was sitting in the masjid along with Mhalasapathy, a rich gentleman came with his family for Baba's darshan. Seeing the ladies in purdah, Nana thought of getting up and leaving to give them enough space and greater freedom. But Baba told him to remain seated peacefully. The family went up and bowed to Baba. One of the ladies raised her veil while bowing. Seeing her incredible beauty, Nana was smitten. He longed to see her face again and again. At the same time, he was ashamed to have such feelings in front of Baba. So he did not raise his head, but the eyes strayed. The omniscient Baba knew Nana's inner state of turmoil and told him:

> Nana, why is your mind disturbed? Let the senses behave according to their inherent nature. Do not interfere. There is no harm in it.

Chapter 49, verse 158

Brahma Deva has created this beautiful world and it is our duty to appreciate its beauty, otherwise the creation will lose its value and charm. The mind will get steady and calm, slowly and gradually.

Chapter 49, verse 159

When the front door is open, why go by the

Sense Control

> backdoor? Where there is a pure heart, there is no difficulty, whatsoever.
>
> Chapter 49, verse 160

> If there is no evil thought in us, why should we be afraid of anyone? The eyes may do their work. Then why should you be embarrassed?
>
> Chapter 49, verse 161

From these words it is evident that it is the thoughts and intentions which result in subsequent actions. If we do not ponder over objects or harbour sensual desires no downfall will come to us.

Hemadpant further explains Baba's words:

> The mind is wavering by nature, but do not let it be unrestrained. Even if the senses are agitated, do not let the body be impatient.
>
> Chapter 49, verse 170

> Senses cannot be trusted. Do not crave for sense pleasures. Gradually, by steady practice, the frivolity will disappear.
>
> Chapter 49, verse 171

> Do not become a slave to the senses. They do not remain suppressed all the time. They should be systematically controlled, considering the circumstances.
>
> Chapter 49, verse 172

> Making the mind desireless observe God's creation. Then senses will be easily controlled and one would forget the enjoyment of senses.
>
> Chapter 49, verse 174

Hemadpant compares the body to a chariot, senses to horses, mind to rein, intellect to the charioteer and the pleasures to roads. The intellect must remain always aware of the attraction of the senses and control them by pulling the rein or the mind.

With the help of a discriminating charioteer, who keeps the reins in hand with discernment, then the horses (or the senses) will not go astray, not even in dreams.

Chapter 49, verse 181

Conclusion

Sensual pleasures lead to physical, moral and spiritual downfall. We should develop a discriminative intellect regarding demerits of indulgence in sensual pleasures. We should develop mental purity and resort to guru and God. We should realise the greatness of human birth and use the body and inner instruments (mind and intellect) for achieving self-realisation. That is the greatest achievement a human being can have, because all other achievements are ephemeral. Sensual pleasures are equal for both human beings and animals. Indulgences in sensual pleasures will only exaggerate the desires and we may waste the precious human life which is meant for God consciousness and self-realisation.

DISPASSION

Even if one acquires detachment, if it is not accompanied by discretion, it is useless. Therefore, honour the vibhuti.
Chapter 33, verse 19

Completely stopping the desire for the fruits of action is the best way for foregoing the desires. Perform your daily routines and specially prescribed duties. This is called the laws of conduct.
Chapter 1, verse 100

Self-control and detachment, if combined together, will take him across the worldly ocean without difficulty, even though he may be a dullard like a millstone.
Chapter 17 verse 42

The Lord has six divine perfections or attributes. Detachment is the first and foremost. Those who are extremely fortunate, they only obtain it and others do not.
Chapter 17, verse 43

He who discards the fruits of action and expectations with the help of full concentration of mind and surrenders to a guru wholeheartedly, then the guru accepts him.
Chapter 17, verse 47

DISPASSION

Disinterested in the fruit of action in the present world and the other world, and unconcerned over the duality of happiness and unhappiness, only the intelligent people enjoy the divine experience.

Chapter 17, verse 102

The literal meaning of the word 'dispassion' is the state or quality of being unemotional or emotionally uninvolved. In spirituality, it means the inner attitude of detachment from worldly affairs and firm belief in the existence and supremacy of the Paramatman. Dispassion is the foremost requirement to progress on the path of spirituality. If we participate in all activities without fostering the idea of doership and enjoyer, we can cross the ocean of worldly existence and reach the other shore of self-realisation. But unless and until the impermanent nature of material existence is firmly imprinted on our mind, we cannot become detached from worldly affairs.

The human mind has a strong affinity for the visible world and it is extremely difficult for it to comprehend the Paramatman, which is the invisible moving force pervading the visible world. There are only two ways to grasp this fact – self-enquiry and company of saints. Realisation of the Paramatman by self-enquiry does not happen in the ordinary course. King Janaka, King Rishabha and Lord Buddha attained self-realisation by self-enquiry. But for all of us, the only way is to resort to the feet of holy masters or saints.

Baba always emphasised that only by dispassion can we walk on the path of spirituality. Discriminative thinking between permanent and impermanent is the prerequisite for development of dispassion. Baba gave Udi, the ash from his dhuni, to imprint this fact on the minds of his devotees.

Hemadpant describes the unreal nature of material existence by comparing it to a tree. A person who realises this truth will not harbour any passion for it.

The Tree of Material Existence

A tree is unperceivable in the initial phase when it exists invisibly inside the seed. After sometime the seed germinates and grows into a tree. Later it can be cut or it perishes by itself. So, in the beginning and end it was non-visible and hence unperceivable. The existence which is perceived in the middle is illusory because it is perishable. In the same way human existence is also illusory. Before the birth of a human body, it is invisible. After death, it again becomes invisible. The existence in the middle is perceivable but it is illusory and unreal, just like a tree. Countless such beings constitute the visible world.

Hemadpant compares the mundane existence to the trunk of a plantain tree which is devoid of pith (essence). The roots of the tree of mundane existence cling to desires for water. Its origin is from actions and desires rooted in ignorance and its nature is of calamity. Its support is the body consciousness. It is full of juices of pairs of opposites. Its expanse is in the belongings and possessions like money, food, children and spouse. Its leaves are shrutis and sprouts are primary sensations. Actions and sublime impressions are its branches. Rituals and charity are the flowers which impart glory to it. Its fruits are the never-ending (cycle of births–deaths). This tree has the character of undergoing a change every moment. From moment to moment it spreads as more branches sprout. Sometimes from a distance they look beautiful, but if embraced, it is found to be prickly. The appearance of this tree is really within Brahman. Brahman, which is of the nature of effulgence (brilliance or radiance), is its pure support. To realise and merge with its pure support, we have to cut down this material existence which is of unreal, unsteady and essence-less nature. The only effective weapon to cut this tree is the sword of detachment.

From this description it is evident that what we consider as desirable is in reality illusory and meaningless. With dispassion and mental renunciation, we should cross the ocean of worldly existence. Saints are the boats which help us to cross the worldly existence. By giving Udi, Baba reminds the devotees to be dispassionate and detached and to seek the Paramatman even while engaging in active mundane life.

Udi

When Baba arrived in Shirdi, he started to live in an old dilapidated masjid. He established the dhuni in the masjid. Dhuni is a small pit in which firewood is burnt and ash is formed and represents the sacrificial fire. The ash from this dhuni is called Udi. Baba gave this Udi to his devotees as prasad. Udi is also called vibhuti or bhasma. In *Shri Gurucharitra*, chapter 29 contains the description of the greatness of bhasma. In verse 253, it is stated:

The greatness of the bhasma is indeed divine. It has particular significance if one receives the bhasma from the guru's hands.

Baba's Udi bestows all kinds of prosperity and protection on devotees. It has disease-curing property also.

But the real purpose of giving Udi was to enable people to think discriminately – to discriminate between what is real and what is unreal. The visible is unreal and Paramatman is real. The body is perishable, the atman is imperishable. The ultimate fate of the visible universe, including the body, is to become a heap of dust and ashes. Baba wants his devotees to remember this eternal truth and live in this world accordingly. Baba wants them to live happily in this world but, at the same time, they must always be aware of the real goal of human life. When they realise that everything which they consider as their own is unreal and transitory, then they will seek the real and the permanent. The Udi symbolises this fact.

Symbolic Meaning of Udi

Baba asked dakshina from his devotees and advised sense-control. This was done to nurture detachment in the devotees. Along with it, Udi was given to cultivate discriminatory thinking. Hemadpant describes the symbolic meaning of 'Udi' as follows:

> The entire universe is full of Maya. Brahman is the only reality, while the universe is illusory. Bear this in mind that this is what the Udi teaches.
>
> Chapter 33, verse 14

> No person belongs to anyone in this world – be they wife, son, uncles or nephews. Naked you came and naked you will return. The Udi is a reminder of it.
>
> Chapter 33, verse 15

> This world is like the Udi. This is the real importance of Udi. Bear this in mind and you will realise it one day.
>
> Chapter 33, verse 24

Like the drops of water on the petals of the lotus, this evanescent body will fall, therefore abandon all pride in it. The giving of Udi' showed this.

Chapter 33, verse 25

This expanse of the whole universe is like a rangoli design drawn with ashes. Think about the illusory nature of the world and the reality abides only in the Udi.

Chapter 33, verse 26

Udi is only dust. All existence which has name and form, ultimately reaches the same state. Whatever changes are observed in the world, they are only for name's sake. This is experienced from the never changing qualities of dust.

Chapter 33, verse 27

If this Udi is applied to the body, then physical and mental sufferings are cured. But the true significance of the Udi is deep and it is meant for discriminatory detachment.

Chapter 33, verse 16

Baba advised his devotees to perform their prescribed duties in a detached manner so that the actions and their effects would not bind them. They should be egoless and be devoid of pride. When they mentally renounce the doership of all actions and surrender them at the feet of Baba, everything will be felt as auspicious occurrences. Then they will not be affected by guilt, dejection, sorrow, happiness or excitement. Thus, they can easily cross the worldly ocean and attain spiritual progress. In Satcharita, in chapter 51, Hemadpant describes an incident which highlights how Baba imparted this learning to a devotee.

Baba's Advice to Pundalika Rao

Pundalika Rao and some of his acquaintances went from Nanded to Rajamundri to meet the great Saint Shri Vasudevananda Saraswati who was also known as Thembe Swami. They had Swami's darshan. During conversation, Shirdi was mentioned and Swami asked them to convey his salutations and request to Baba, whenever they happened to go there. Swami entrusted a coconut with them to be given to Baba.

Within a month, Pundalika Rao had an opportunity to go to Shirdi, along with four of his friends. When they reached Manmad railway station, there was still some time for the departure of the train to Kopergaon. They were thirsty and so they went to a nearby river. In order to avoid drinking water on an empty stomach, one of them took out a small bundle of chivada which he was carrying. Since it was very pungent and spicy, someone suggested to mix coconut with the chivada. Unknowingly, they broke the same coconut which was entrusted to Pundalika Rao by Thembe Swami. When Pundalika Rao came to know about this, he became dejected and remorseful. When they reached Shirdi, Pundalika Rao went for Baba's darshan. Baba, on his own, told him, 'Bring me the article which you have brought from my brother.'

Pundalika Rao confessed that they had eaten the coconut. He pleaded Baba for forgiveness and told him that he would bring another coconut. Baba stopped him and said:

> The worth of that fruit could not be matched by giving any number of others. Whatever had to happen, has happened. Why unnecessarily brood over it?
>
> Chapter 51, verse 175

It was only by my resolve that the Swami gave you the coconut and that the fruit was broken by my volition. Why do you unnecessarily take the doership?

Chapter 51, verse 176

You are feeling guilty because you have an ego. Just be egoless. You will be free from all guilt.

Chapter 51, verse 177

Why is there pride in doing a good or meritorious deed? And why does one shirk away from a sinful one? The result of both is the same! Therefore, act without the sense of doership.

Chapter 51, verse 178

It occurred to me that you should see me. Therefore, the coconut was entrusted into your hands. This is the truth.

Chapter 51, verse 179

After all you are my children. The fruit that you have eaten is as good as being offered to me. Believe that I have definitely received it.

Chapter 51, verse 180

When Pundalika Rao understood this, then his mind calmed down. With Sai's words his anxiety dissolved gradually. By this incident Baba is teaching his devotees how to behave in mundane life so that they can attain the goal of spirituality instead of being immersed in the fearful worldly existence.

Conclusion
In Satcharita, Hemadpant gives the message of living egoless and surrendering wholeheartedly at the feet of guru.

I am not the doer of any action nor the enjoyer of its fruits. When I feel this, this is an action which is devoid of ego and is the surrender to the Supreme Being for union with it.

Chapter 1, verse 97

Perform all your actions in this way. Then, naturally, a stage is reached when you become a non-doer. Though it is not possible ever to disown karma, yet it is possible to disown the fruit of the karma.

Chapter 1, verse 98

To lead our life in such a manner, we need to have full faith in the guru's words and be of resolute mind. We should control our mind, intellect and other senses and use them for acquiring knowledge of self. We should realise that God pervades the world of names and forms, from inside and outside, the all-pervading spirit, devoid of any particular shape. This ordinary material world of beings, movable and immovable objects, should not be taken into account at all. We should have full faith in God, who is the Supreme One. If we cannot comprehend this concept about this world and its nature, then at least we should try and give up the passion for accumulation of wealth, gold and so on. Even if this is impossible to practise, then remember that we only have a right to action, not of the fruits of the actions.

All this should always be practised in accordance with the doctrines prescribed by the scriptures as per our station in life to make the intellect pure. Hemadpant advises devotees to completely surrender the vacillating mind at Sai's feet. Then Sai will be the doer of actions that arise by his inspiration. Similarly, the initiative and energy to act should also be completely surrendered to Sai. We should behave according to his will, leaving all the burden on him performing all our actions without pride.

DEVOTION

Even though the body is perishable, it is a means towards gaining enlightenment, which is readily more desirable than salvation, because through it, we can experience bhakti.

Chapter 24, verse 60

This fifth rung of gaining enlightenment is superior to the other four – kama, artha, dharma and moksha. They cannot be compared to bhakti. Invaluable are the gains of bhakti.

Chapter 24, verse 61

One who achieves fulfilment by serving the guru can fully understand the implications of this statement. They alone will achieve enlightenment by understanding the inherent meaning of bhakti – knowledge and detachment.

Chapter 24, verse 62

8

DEVOTION

> There is no need to be well-versed in the Vedas nor any need to be famous as a scholar. It is neither necessary to sing the praises of God without feeling. Only the loving sentiment of devotion is essential.
>
> Chapter 21, verse 98

Devotion or bhakti is an internal feeling. It is an emotion derived from relationship with God. Hemadpant says:

> Whatever the attachment for different objects, if all such love is collected and poured in a mould at the feet of the Lord, then it appears in the form of devotion.
>
> Chapter 10, verse 128

People seek divine help mainly to fulfil desires or when they become totally helpless in life. Only a few people, who are highly knowledgeable, seek divinity because of their wisdom tells them to do so. When a person loves God unconditionally without any motives, there arises pure devotion. Many devotional movements and sects are present in India.

This world and all creatures are manifestations of one infinite consciousness, which is called Paramatman. It is present in the world and all the creations. At the same time, it exists independently of them. In its independent existence, it is omnipotent, omniscient and limitless. When it gets embodied, it has varying degrees of limitations and qualities. In some objects it is inert, in some it is mobile and in some it is static. In mobile bodies, some are vocal and some are not vocal. Likewise, in some lands, consciousness is conducive to enjoy material comforts, in some lands it is conducive to poverty, in some lands it is conducive to spiritual advancement.

Sacred scriptures praise Bharatam as one which is conducive to practising devotion to God. They call it as 'Jambu Dweepa' and its religion as one which helps to achieve self-realisation. The people inhabiting this land will be able to realise the purpose of human life and achieve liberation if they practise their religious duties and be devoted to God. Bharatam always had an unbroken line of preceptors, sages, saints and devotional movements. 'By getting a birth in Bharatam and living there, spiritual realisation can easily be achieved' – if anyone thinks so, it is a mistake. If we desire to achieve spiritual progress, we should be ready to do hard work and toil incessantly. The most valuable and desirable thing which a human being should achieve is the realisation of Paramatman and being in union with it. That precious thing cannot be achieved so easily. Baba says, 'He will reap as he sows.'

There are two ways of realisation of Paramatman – one is knowledge and the other is devotion (bhakti). Realising the Paramatman through knowledge is an appropriate and worthy way. But except for very wise and selfless souls, this mode is prone to downfall. Those who try to realise Paramatman through intellectual exercises are often sidetracked by their doubts and confusions. This method is not suitable for common people who form the majority and who do not know anything except family, relations and various vexations. For them Baba advised the path of devotion.

Greatness of Devotion

Hemadpant describes both paths (knowledge and bhakti) in Chapter 19.

> Although knowledge is the best of all, which Baba preached day and night, even then for the ordinary people, he advocated the path of devotion.
>
> Chapter 19, verse 25

> He talked of the greatness of the path of knowledge which was like the ramphal (bullock's heart fruit) and the path of devotion was like eating sitaphal (custard apple), which is simple and sweet.
>
> Chapter 19, verse 26

> Devotion is like a pure sitaphal and knowledge is like a ripened ramphal, one juicier than the other, both with exquisite fragrance.
>
> Chapter 19, verse 27

> He who waits to let the ramphal ripen on the tree finds it tastes very sweet; but if the pulp of the ramphal is tasted when the fruit is taken raw from the tree and then ripened, it tastes sharp.
>
> Chapter 19, verse 28

> The taste of the ramphal is sweeter when it starts ripening on the stem of the tree. If it falls on the ground it tastes sharp. It becomes very sweet if it ripens on the tree.
>
> Chapter 19, verse 29

> Whoever knows to ripen it on the tree, he alone can enjoy the sweet taste of it. But a sitaphal does not require such efforts. Still, it has good qualities and is also precious.
>
> Chapter 19, verse 30

Ramphal has the fear of falling down and even for a person who is in pursuit of knowledge, there is always the fear of falling from grace. He must conquer the eight siddhis and should not neglect this even for a little while.

Chapter 19, verse 31

Therefore Sai, the cloud of mercy, often explained to his disciples about the importance of devotion and chanting of God's name.

Chapter 19, verse 32

A person who is following the path of knowledge for self-realisation will be tormented by his own intellectual notions and predicaments. Through yogic practices he comes to know about the workings of physical elements, internal forces and their interactions. Thus, he acquires supernatural powers. These powers distract him from the goal unless he is very vigilant. So, this path is compared to ramphal. He should always be vigilant so that he is not knocked down by supernatural powers, which is similar to the premature falling down of the ramphal. He should not try to reach the goal without exercising the required efforts – otherwise the taste will be sharp as if eating an unripe ramphal. He should be diligent in his efforts and patiently wait till his efforts mature into self-realisation in their natural course. He should drive away all internal and external disturbances and temptations to achieve the goal, that is, he should know how to keep the ramphal on the tree itself till it becomes ripe. That is why Baba stressed the importance and greatness of devotion. Devotion is like sitaphal, it does not need strenuous intellectual or mental efforts. Even if sitaphal falls prematurely, its taste and sweetness do not alter. Likewise, even if a devotee is imperfect on his path, he will never be in dilemma.

Devotion

When we love God unconditionally, with a pure heart and depend on him totally, like an innocent child depends on its mother, then God gives himself to us. God comes to reside in our heart and makes us realise him – because God resides in truth, in a clear heart and a clear mind.

In this regard the story of Anandarao Patankar, described in Chapter 21 of Satcharita, is very apt. Patankar had learnt all Vedas, Vedangas, Upanishads and other holy scriptures and commentaries. But his mind always remained restless and despondent. Peace of mind eluded him. He came for Baba's darshan and humbly told him about his condition. He said:

> All my study of books, learning of shastras is a waste. All this bookish knowledge is futile as long as my mind remains unsteady. How empty is the effort I have made over the study of etymology! To what purpose is the japa and mantra which does not give peace of mind? How will I then ever acquire the knowledge of Brahman?
>
> Chapter 21, verses 80, 81

Baba replied to him with a parable:

> Once a merchant came, and at that time a horse passed nine balls of stool in front of him. The merchant was very efficient. He immediately took off his wrap, and spread it out, collected all the balls and tied a knot and was able to achieve concentration of mind.
>
> Chapter 21 verses 87, 88

Later, Dada Kelkar explained the meaning of that parable to Patankar:

> The horse is God's grace. The nine balls of stool represent navavidha bhakti. Without devotion one

cannot have union with God and knowledge will not be acquired.

Chapter 21, verse 94

Hemadpant says:

With full faith even if one of these ways of devotion is practised, Shri Hari who longs for devotion will appear in the home of the devotee.

Chapter 21, verse 96

Paramatman is Pure Consciousness and omnipotent intelligence. He is formless. The world arises in that consciousness as a result of a momentary conceptualisation and exists as a reflection in it. The world and its activities are dependent on that Pure Consciousness; but the Pure Consciousness is independent. This Pure Consciousness is known as Nirakara Brahman. To grasp the formless Pure Consciousness as Paramatman and be in union with it is very difficult for most people. People can easily concentrate on concrete forms rather than abstract concepts. By worshipping concrete forms like idols, fire, water, sun and so on, the mind gets controlled and concentrated. Practising worship of forms for a prolonged period enables people to realise the formless Pure Consciousness. That is why Baba advised devotional worship by adopting any of the nine ways of bhakti.

Nine Ways of Devotional Worship (Navavidha Bhakti)

Many different types of worship enable the devotees to utilise human qualities to achieve union with God. All these modes of worship are applicable for worshipping our guru also. The nine ways of worship described in Satcharita are the following:

1. *Shravanam*: Listening to God's stories and leelas.

Baba encouraged his devotees to read and listen to sacred texts and religious discourses. Bapu Saheb Jog used to recite *Jnaneswari* and other holy texts and devotees used to listen to him regularly.

2. *Kirthanam*: Musical chanting of Lord's names, stories and leelas.

   When the mind is completely absorbed in singing the praises of God, it becomes one with him. Baba's great devotee Das Ganu had dedicated his life for this way of worship. He became a Haridasa, following the tradition of Narada. He performed kirthanam in and around Mumbai and innumerable people were benefitted.

3. *Smaranam*: Remembrance of God.

   Constant remembrance of God purifies the consciousness and enables us for God realisation. Continuous naamajapa sustains the remembrance of God. Baba encouraged devotees to conduct week-long chanting of holy names.

4. *Pada seva*: Worship by submitting at the feet of the Lord.

   For getting to God, submitting oneself with body and mind and doing service is the fourth way of bhakti. Even more meritorious is to submit at the feet of the guru. Without guru, it is impossible to even have a glimpse of Paramatman. Baba advised His devotees to serve their respective gurus, unmindful of any difficulties.

5. *Archana*: Offering of flowers, sacred leaves, clothes, food, jewellery, etc. to God.

   Baba was very particular that devotees should continue their respective traditional devotional practices. Megha was a great devotee of Baba. He considered Baba as Lord Shiva. Every day he used to worship all village deities and then come to the masjid to perform Baba's worship. One day he could not open the Khandoba temple. So, he went directly to the masjid. Omniscient Baba told him that he had missed Khandoba's worship and that the door was now open. He sent Megha to complete the ritual.

Bhagavantrao Ksheerasagar's father was a devotee of Pandharpur Vittal. After his death his family members stopped the worship and the annual pilgrimage. Baba reminded Bhagavantrao to continue with the worship.

6. *Vandanam*: Prostrations before the Lord, sages, saints, guru, learned people, elders and so on.

Worshipping by prostration is the easiest form of worship, but it should be done with the fullest faith and unflinching belief. By offering prostrations we become humble and lose pride and ego. Baba advised his devotees that the atman is residing in every being and hence they should be humble and love all equally, irrespective of any differences. This will be equal to mental prostrations to every being.

7. *Dasyam*: Having a relationship of master and servant with the Lord.

Here the devotee serves the Lord as a servant. Building and renovating temple and lodgings for devotees, organising religious festivals, etc. are done as a servant, on behalf of the Lord. The same service mentality should be offered to the Lord's devotees also. Kaka Saheb Dikshit is an eminent example of this type of bhakti. He served Baba with his body, mind and his entire wealth.

8. *Sakhyam*: Having an attitude of friendship with God.

We should make friends with God and bind him with friendship and love. If our feelings towards the Lord are so intense that we forget everything else except God, and if there is no one except God for us, then God will be our most readily available friend, philosopher and guide, who will come to our help without being called, at the right time and the right place.

Arjuna had developed devotion to Lord Krishna through friendship. The Lord, in turn, even drove Arjuna's chariot during the Kurukshetra War. Anyone who develops such an intense bhakti towards God or guru can also get God or guru themselves as the charioteer of his life. Madhavarao Deshpande developed sakhyabhakti towards Baba. Once Baba told him that he and Madhavarao were together for seventy-two lives!

9. *Atmanivedanam*: Total surrender to the Lord.

Atmanivedanam bhakti is submitting ourselves totally and wholly in all aspects to God, leaving everything to him as far as we are concerned. The complete and total disappearance of our own body and mind state is the real submission to God. The baseless pride about our body and mind should be discarded. When the body and mental senses are dissolved, there will not be any 'I' state. Then there will be no difference between the devotee and the Lord. Worship by total submission to God is by far the best, for obvious reasons as it can be performed only after we are able to attain the real knowledge and are prepared to work further for Paramatman.

Megha was a selfless devotee who had submitted his entire self to Baba. Baba helped him in all ways for his spiritual progress. When Megha left this world, Baba was seen to be overwhelmed with grief; he was wailing as loudly as any other mortal being would. Baba followed the funeral procession and offered flowers on the body.

Baba always promoted devotional practices, according to the devotee's belief systems, whether they belonged to Hindu or Muslim religion. He did not promote any particular sect. All he said was that practice of true bhakti and real yearning for God will definitely take the devotee to the goal.

If a person has true devotion and intense inner feeling, he can get God realisation at the same spot where he resides. Once Baba asked Das Ganu to conduct a seven-day chanting of God's name and Das Ganu wanted a confirmation that Vittal would appear in person after the completion of chanting. Baba replied:

> Dankapuri of Dakurnath or Pandhari of Vittal or Dwarakanagari of Ranchod are here only, in search of which you need not go a long distance.
>
> Chapter 4, verse 85

> Is Vittal going to come from anywhere else, leaving his private quarters? He will appear here, springing up out of the intense devotion of the devotee.
>
> Chapter 4, verse 86

After seven days of chanting, Baba's words came true and Das Ganu had darshan of Lord Vittal in Shirdi.

Kaka Saheb Received Darshan of Vittal

On another occasion, when Kaka Saheb Dixit was in meditation, he had darshan of Vittal. Later, when he went for Baba's darshan, Baba asked him, 'Had not Vittal Patil come? Did you meet him?'

> That Vittal is very elusive. Hold to him firmly otherwise he will slip away if your attention wavers even for a moment.
>
> Chapter 4, verse 91

On the same day, in the afternoon, a hawker brought around twenty-five pictures of Vittal for selling. Dixit lovingly bought one picture and started worshipping it.

Nana Chandorkar and Darshan of Datta

Once Nana Chandorkar came to Shirdi with his brother-in-law. After paying obeisance to Sainath, both of them sat in front of him. While they were exchanging generalities about the welfare and well-being, Baba suddenly got angry. He said, 'Nana how is it that you have forgotten? After having spent such a long time in my company, is this only what you have learnt? Is this the result of the time you have spent in my company? How could your judgement have strayed like this? Tell me in detail.'

Listening to this Nana became dejected. He could not remember where he had erred. He could not find any reason for the anger. Therefore, he held Baba's feet and repeatedly entreated him to tell him the reason. Baba asked him what had happened on the way while he reached Kopergaon. Nana narrated everything in detail. They had hired a tonga to come straight to Shirdi. When they reached Kopergaon, his brother-in-law wanted to go to the Dutta temple and take the Lord's darshan. Since he was in a hurry and he thought it would get late in reaching Shirdi, Nana discouraged him saying that they could take the darshan on their return journey. Later, while bathing in the Godavari river, a big thorn pierced his foot and gave him a lot of trouble on the way, till he pulled it out with much effort. Baba replied, 'It is not good to be in such haste. Thank your stars that you had only the thorn to contend with, though you had disrespected the darshan. When a very venerated deity like Dutta is on the way, awaiting darshan, unfortunate is he who has not taken the darshan. How can I help such a person?' How wonderful is Baba's method of instruction and love for his devotees!

Considering God in different forms and adoring and pouring out pure and unconditional love at his feet by practising navavidha bhakti take the devotee to the greatest realms of fulfilment and satisfaction. But practising such devotion is also not easy. Hemadpant says:

> The four-fold path of karma (action), jnanam (knowledge), yoga (yogic powers) and bhakti (devotion), though each is distinct from the other, all lead to the same goal.
>
> Chapter 6, verse 15
>
> The path of bhakti is the thorny path, like the path through a prickly babul forest. It is full of pits and potholes. Just one or two steps, in the right direction, takes you really close to God.
>
> Chapter 6, verse 16
>
> You should avoid the thorns and step forward. You will reach the destination without fear. This is the only remedy, says the Gurumayi very clearly.
>
> Chapter 6, verse 17

On the path of devotion, mental impurities and bodily demands are the thorns and pits. Greed, pride, sectarian thinking, jealousy, contentiousness and so on are the mental impediments. Desire for enjoying pleasures, laziness, addiction to tasty foods, sleep, etc. are other impediments. Devotees should be cautious to avoid undesirable tendencies.

Conclusion

By practising devotion to God and guru, normal people who are bound to family life can easily progress towards acquiring real knowledge provided they are earnest in their

Devotion

efforts and have staunch faith. By practising navavidha bhakti, the devotee achieves concentration, mental peace and union with the worshipped. Hemadpant says:

> When the orchard of mind is watered by devotion, detachment will grow, knowledge will blossom, union with the Supreme Spirit comes to fruition and joy will burst forth, avoiding the cycle of births and deaths as a certainty.
>
> Chapter 6, verse 18

LOVE

If someone loves me more than life, I need such a person. If such a person gives me something, I give him a hundred-fold.
Chapter 14, verse 95

Once when one sees him with love, then he becomes his slave for the rest of his life. He is hungry only for the singular love and responds to the call of such a person.
Chapter 33, verse 132

Irrespective of whether a devotee is full of faith or mocking, he is equally merciful to both. This loving mother did not differentiate between both.
Chapter 35, verse 127

One should keep permanent peace and happiness as one's goal of life and think about it. Serve all beings as God – this is the most beneficial faith in life.
Chapter 8, verse 31

People meet as destiny decides. We come together because of good fortune. We should therefore nurture affection for each other and enjoy happiness and serenity.
Chapter 19, verse 150

9

LOVE

> I am under my devotees' obligations. I am always beside them. I am always hungry for love. I am at their beck and call.
>
> Chapter 11, verse 76

Love is an abstract reality. In the physical world people usually interpret love as an emotional feeling which has only a mental realm. Their concept of love includes affection and liking, which are felt between people during interpersonal relations. Their love includes maternal and paternal love, fraternal love, love between couples, infatuation and love between companions and friends. All these types of love are conditioned by mental notions and ideas. They are driven by ego. The idea of 'I' and 'mine' creates attachment and liking. So, such love is based on selfishness. People try to possess what they think is desirable and reject the undesirable. Love in mundane life is based on a give-and-take policy. It is within the constraints of physical and emotional factors. So, it cannot be considered as true and ideal.

Love in the Spiritual Sense

Love in the spiritual sense has a broad meaning. It is an inner virtue by which we feel unconditional and selfless affection, concern, compassion and mercy for another living being. It is not at all driven by ego or conditioned by external factors. It springs from the realisation that one undivided consciousness fills all beings and all are the essential part of that One. There is no feeling of 'I' and 'mine', 'you' and 'yours'. Such beings see no division or duality. They see themselves in all. Such persons feel the pain of others as their own. They feel happiness when other persons are happy. Such great souls identify themselves with all creatures. This is called universal love.

Such universal love is possible only by a God-realised soul. That is why it is said that God is love. Shri Shirdi Sai Baba is Parabrahman incarnate. His mission was to spread the message of universal love. Incarnations happen according to the need of the respective times. Earlier incarnations happened mainly to abolish unrighteousness, oppression and aggression, as those of Lord Narasimha, Lord Shri Rama, Lord Shri Krishna, Lord Parasurama and so on. In Kaliyuga, Paramatman incarnates as gurus. Kaliyuga is the age of darkness, vices and rivalry and the guru shows the right path.

In *Bhagavatapuranam*, there is a description of how Kali enters the earth. King Parikshit, on seeing Kali who was disguised as a lowly man attired in royal dress, raised his sword to kill him. But Kalipurusha took refuge at the king's feet and so the king forgave him and asked him to leave his country. But Kali requested him for some places where he could dwell. King Parikshit allowed him to live in gambling dens, in brothels, in wine shops and in slaughter houses. Kali requested him to allot some more places where he could dwell. The king told him to live in gold, pride, passion, ignorance and enmity.

In the present times, Kali has spread its influence on the whole world. All people are immersed in ignorance and vicious qualities. Enmity, quarrel, sectarianism and contentiousness are prevalent everywhere. So, in the present age, Paramatman incarnates as knowledge, love, harmony, truth, compassion and mercy through realised masters. They spread this message to the humanity through their own lives. They do not give long discourses or sermons. Their way of living itself is their message. Because of their inner realisation, they see the whole world as an extension of their self. They see only the pure consciousness everywhere. So, for them everything in this world is pure. They see only harmony and unity.

Baba advised his devotees to forget differences and love one another. He told them to love the weak and the sick and to give all possible services to them. He advised forgiveness. The vicious qualities like hatred, malice and enmity are hindrances to mental evolution and spiritual progress. He advised the devotees to love and be compassionate, not only towards fellow beings but also towards all creatures. When people have selfless love for all creatures, it is equal to serving the Paramatman. When a person loves fellow beings, the Lord personally manifests in his heart. Because of the inner purity, the person receives all favourable circumstances for realisation of self.

Baba's Universal Love

Baba loved all creatures. He said many times that he resided in all of them. His love for humans and all other creatures was like a mother's love for her children. He said that his masjid is Dwarakamayi. Dwaraka is one of the seven places of liberation. Mayi means mother. He assured his devotees that whoever steps into the masjid would be relieved of all worries. Once he forewarned Balasaheb Mirikar about an impending danger. At that time he said:

> This is our Dwarakamayi. When sitting in the lap of the masjid, she safeguards the children and there will never be any question of worrying.
>
> Chapter 22, verse 48

This Masjidmayi is very kind. She is the mother of all innocent and faithful devotees. Anyone may face any difficulty, she will readily protect.
Chapter 22, verse 49

Once a person settles in her lap, all his difficulties are solved. He who lies in her shadow, will be on the throne of happiness.
Chapter 22, verse 50

Baba loved all and protected all. Sometimes he was like a mother bird who protected all her chicklings by keeping them under her wings. For some other children, he was a mother tortoise. There is no apparent direct external exchange of nourishment, but mother tortoise's merciful glances are always on her children who are on the other shore. Tortoise children's only means of sustenance is their memory of their mother. Mother tortoise's merciful glances and her children's memory of their mother and total inner dependence are enough for those children's life, growth, and protection.

Sai Satcharita is a testimonial of Baba's universal love. All incidents depicted in Sai Satcharita are, in fact, the depiction of Baba's love for his devotees and all other beings. Baba knew about the hunger of a stray dog, an innocent child's impending fall in a furnace and his devotees' unspoken ailments, wishes and worries. His love and concern for his devotees were not confined to their present life, but had been present throughout their many previous lives too. Even though some people, because of their actions, fell from highest form of human life to a lower form, Baba kept his promise of giving them protection and salvation.

Baba's Unity with All Creatures

Baba was a brahmachari and also a sanyasi. He lived by begging. He placed the food thus received in a pot in the masjid. Dogs, crows, cats, all ate from that pot. He never drove them away.

Once Mrs Tarkad was in Shirdi. While she was in the kitchen and leaf-plates were set for the meal in the afternoon, a hungry dog came to the door. When she was about to give a piece of the bhakari which was in her plate to the dog, a pig bespattered with mud, arrived there, looking very hungry. She fed both the animals in the normal course and did not give any importance to the incident. But when she went to the masjid, Baba told her that she satisfied his hunger by giving him bhakari, which was actually given to the dog and the pig. He told her:

> Know that this is the kindness which I preach.
> Give food to the hungry first and then eat yourself.
> Remember this clearly in your mind.
>
> Chapter 9, verse 122

Baba told her that he is one with all creatures – dogs, pigs, cows, cats, ants, flies, fish and so on. He said:

> That person who sees me in all the creatures, you must understand, is my beloved one. Give up the belief in the two-fold nature, and worship me in this manner.
>
> Chapter 9, verse 130

Baba loved all people irrespective of whether they were rich or poor, affluent or impoverished, high caste or low caste. He served sick people. He relieved their pain and discomfort. He fed the poor, the orphans and the beggars. He did not discriminate against anyone.

Baba Saved a Child from the Furnace and a Leper-Devotee's Service to Baba

Once on Dhanteras day in 1910, Baba was sitting near the dhuni and offering small pieces of firewood in it.

The dhuni was very hot and brightly lit up. Suddenly, he inserted his hand into the fire. Madhav and Madhavarao ran towards him immediately and pulled him back. They were worried and asked him what did he do. Baba told them that a blacksmith's child suddenly slipped into the furnace. The mother was carrying the child on her waist. She transferred the child to her arm and started blowing the bellows of the furnace. Hearing her husband calling, she got frightened. In her anxiety, she forgot that the child was in her arms. The child was extremely restless and slipped into the furnace. While Baba was trying to take her out of the furnace, his arm got scorched. Baba said that he was not bothered about the burns but about the child's safety.

Baba allowed only the leper-devotee Bhagoji Shinde to tender to his burnt arm. Bhagoji used to apply ghee, place a leaf upon it and tightly bandage it every day. Baba did not allow Dr Paramanand to examine his arm or treat it. Even though the arm healed completely and there was no pain, Bhagoji continued to apply ghee and massage it regularly, apparently for no reason. The service was for the sake of Bhagoji. Sai Baba did not need it. He made Bhagoji render regular service with love as a devotee should. Because of his numerous earlier sins, Bhagoji was afflicted with leprosy. But he was foremost in his service to Baba. He derived four-fold happiness from his service. Baba allowed him to continue with his service for the benefit his devotee.

Baba's Loving Concern for His Devotees' Wishes

Baba loved all creatures. He reciprocated in the same measure to those who had pure, unalloyed love for him. Once Mrs Tarkhad sent two brinjals with Mrs Purandare and instructed her to make bharta with one of them and kacharya with the other. After reaching Shirdi, Mrs Purandare prepared bharta for lunch, offered it as naivedya and left for her lodging place. When Baba tasted the bharta, he relished it and shared it with everyone. He then asked for kacharya. But that was not the season for brinjals. So, the devotees went to search for Mrs Purandare as she had brought the bharta. They asked her about the brinjal. Then everyone came to know the significance of the kacharya and Baba's keenness for it. The lady had thought that she would prepare and take the kacharya later, with the next meal. But seeing Baba's response, she prepared the dish quickly and offered it to him.

On another occasion, Mrs Tarkhad sent a pedha with Mankar's son. He was going to Shirdi to perform the last rites of his late father. Mrs Tarkhad felt like sending something for Baba. Since there was nothing else, she could find in the house and the boy was in a hurry, she sent a pedha which had already been offered earlier as naivedya during worship. The boy reached Shirdi and took Baba's darshan. But he had forgotten to take the pedha with him. Baba waited patiently.

In the afternoon also the boy forgot about the pedha. Baba asked him what he had brought for him. The boy replied he had nothing. Then Baba tried to remind him, 'Has no one given you anything for me?' When the boy said 'No,' Sai Samartha questioned him directly, 'When you left home, did not mother give you a sweet lovingly?' Then the boy remembered. He asked for Baba's forgiveness, brought the pedha and gave it to him. As soon as Baba received it, he put it in his mouth and thus gratified the feelings of his devotee.

Dadasaheb Khaparde's Son

Once Shri Khaparde's young son had very high fever. His mother became very anxious and agitated. There was a scare of plague also at that time. So, she thought of going to her home in Amaravati. In the evening, when Baba came near the wade, she bowed down at his feet and told him what had happened. Baba reassured her and showed four buboes of the size of a hen's egg on his waist. He said, 'I have to bear this because of your difficulties.' People were amazed to witness this divine and unique ordeal.

Nanasaheb Chandorkar

Once Nana was posted as Mamlatdar of Pandharpur. He received the order at Nandurbar and was asked to leave immediately. Nana, along with his family, started to Shirdi to pay respects to Baba. Nana did not send a message to anybody about his arrival. Baba was in the masjid with Mhalasapathy, Appa Shinde and Kashiram. Nana must have been in the outskirts of Nimagaon at that time. Suddenly, out of nowhere, Baba said that all of them would sing a bhajan. The main line of the bhajan was, 'I am going to Pandharpur and I will stay there. That is the abode of my master.'

Baba himself sang the bhajan and the devotees followed Him. Nana and his family arrived, bowed down at his feet and requested him to go with them to Pandharpur. Then people informed him that Baba was already ready to go to Pandharpur, as bhajan's words indicated!

Sometimes Baba helped his devotees to fulfil even their unspoken desires as in the case of Mrs Nimonkar. She had to go to Belapur as her son, who was living there, was unwell. Nanasaheb Nimonkar told her that she should return the very next day. But she wanted to spend an extra day there as it was the amavas of the Pola festival. But Nanasaheb did not agree. She made preparations for her journey and went to take Baba's darshan. Baba was standing in front of Sathe wada and was surrounded by a group of devotees including Nanasaheb Nimonkar. When she bowed at his feet, Baba told her to go as early as she could and stay at Belapur for four days at leisure. Baba's words gave unimaginable peace of mind to the lady. Nanasaheb Nimonkar was also satisfied.

Baba Saved the Villagers from Heavy Rainfall and Storms

Once there was a thunderous storm accompanied by heavy rainfall in Shirdi. All the villagers were in panic, seeing the wrath of the nature. They prayed fervently to all the village deities. But none of them came to help. The villagers, cattle, animals, birds, all flocked to the masjid. Seeing the distress of the people, Baba came to the door of the masjid and looking to the sky, he roared. Loud shouts followed one after another, resounding in the sky. Immediately, the storm subsided and it became peaceful. The villagers and other creatures were relieved of the calamity.

Baba's love for his devotees is not confined to the present life. It springs from their numerous previous lives as indicated by Baba to Shama that they were together for seventy-two lives. Baba told Mrs Tarkhad and her son, 'Mark the bonds that we have from the past births!'

Once Baba took the plate of naivedya offered by Mrs Khaparde very eagerly and ate the food with great relish. When the other devotees asked about the reason for this action, Baba described her previous four lives, beginning from a cow.

Even when his devotees had not behaved appropriately and fallen into lower species, he had great love and compassion for them. A tiger who got salvation at Baba's feet, two goats who were brothers in their previous lives, the snake Veerabhadrappa and the frog Channabasappa are a few examples of Baba's love.

Conclusion

Baba advised His devotees to practise selfless love for all creatures by realising that the inner soul of all creatures was the same. He told them to oblige even those who rebuked and harmed them. He said that it is the atman which dwells even in snakes and scorpions and each one acts according to God's will.

Baba said that it is better to always follow non-violence. This does not mean that we should accept everything passively. But we should act with wisdom and discrimination. We should keep ourselves away from enmity and malice. We should keep our inner being at the feet of the guru and God. If we cannot give any monetary help or service to people, we should at least speak kindly to them and pray for the good of all.

Keeping a mind which is clear, pure and full of love will draw both the Almighty and the guru towards a devotee. God is hungry for pure love. He moves away from hypocrites. Pure love for fellow beings and all creatures bestows us God's grace. One who loves guru and God by practising devotion will definitely love all creatures selflessly. Love is the greatest virtue by which Baba's devotees will be able to obtain his grace.

Baba once described how he and his three friends had set out in search of the Brahman. They met a vanjari in the forest and he lovingly offered them food and water. Baba's three friends, who were learned scholars, refused his offer and went away. But Baba accepted the food and water. Baba says:

> He who loves others disinterestedly is really enlightened. I thought acceptance of his hospitality was the best beginning for getting knowledge.

Chapter 32, verse 64

The scholars were learned and knowledgeable and were searching for God. But God manifested in the heart of the vanjari as love and offered food and water for them who were thirsty and hungry after a tedious search for Him. They lacked love for a fellow being and refused his cordial offer. But Baba accepted the food and God manifested as a guru and gave him enlightenment. Love for fellow beings is more conducive for God realisation than intellectual exercise and pride

TRUTHFULNESS

God is the embodiment of his own devotees. He longs for the simple and guileless. He is completely indebted to those who love him, but he shuns the hypocrites.

Chapter 3, verse 9

Always practise truth; listen to the stories about the saints; bow down at the feet of the saints; sins will be washed away.

Chapter 18, verse 26

If anybody is in need of money and you are not desirous of giving, do not give; but at least don't behave in an insulting manner and bark like a dog at him.

Chapter 19, verse 143

He who definitely wishes to escape the bonds of birth and death, should follow the path of righteousness very meticulously and be always tranquil.

Chapter 19, verse 216

TRUTHFULNESS

Even a devotee like Sudama whose friend was Lord Krishna, when he forgot to behave according to the law of good virtuosity, suffered in this world.

Chapter 24, verse 86

Truthfulness means genuineness or honesty. In spirituality, truth is the other name for Paramatman. This means that Paramatman exists in a natural state without any modifications. But jiva or individual consciousness is enmeshed in physical qualities and mental modifications. When we get free from such conditioning and abide in pure consciousness, we become pure and truthful. In mundane life the quality of truthfulness means being honest and sincere in our words, deeds and speech. Such truthfulness is a great virtue. A person who is truthful will have other good human qualities like love, devotion, compassion, mercy, fraternity and so on. Baba had given utmost importance to truthfulness. His life itself is the example. He advised his devotees to be always truthful. When we are truthful, vicious qualities will not occur in us. This will be conducive for leading a life of devotion and spirituality. When we are not living truthfully, we will be leading a life of conceit, greed, pride and jealousy. This will be harmful to ourselves and our fellow beings.

Hemadpant begins the Satcharita by describing an incident of Baba grinding wheat to ward off the disease of cholera. Four women volunteered to grind the wheat and took the peg from his hands. They ground the wheat and gathered almost four seers of flour. Then they thought that Baba was living alone without any family or relatives and also, he did not cook for himself. So they thought the flour could be shared among themselves. They took the flour and prepared to leave. Then Baba asked them, 'Did you give the wheat on loan that you want to take away the flour?' He told them to go to the village boundary and to spread the flour there.

The women had assumed that Baba was staying alone and did not need the flour. So they wanted to take the flour for themselves. They did not even ask his permission whether they could do so. We should maintain truthfulness in all circumstances, whether we are being observed or not by anyone. A truthful person will never take another's property without his permission. Covetousness originate when a person is not truthful and resorts to falsehood.

There are many incidents described in Satcharita which teach us that we should always be truthful.

Oil Merchants Denied Oil to Baba

In his earlier days, Baba used to beg for oil from shops and with that oil, he lighted earthen lamps in temples and masjid. Later the oil merchants did not want to give the oil for free. They decided that from then onwards they would not give oil to Baba. When Baba came to beg for oil, all of them told him that there was no oil. Baba returned to masjid without saying anything and lighted the lamps with water. The oil merchants were dumbfounded. They bowed at Baba's feet and prayed for forgiveness. It is always better to politely tell the truth rather than tell lies or mock the other person.

Truthfulness should be maintained in our speech and thoughts also. Our attitude and behaviour also should always be based on truth. When we deviate from the path of truthfulness, disgrace and misfortune befall on us. Gods will bear all the misfortunes befalling on their devotees, in reciprocation of their devotion. But even these gods are not able to bear the after-effects of untruthfulness. When we deviate from the path of goodness and virtuosity, even if the Lord himself is our friend, we will have to suffer.

In this context, Hemadpant narrates the story of Sudama:

Sudama and the Grams

Sudama was Lord Krishna's childhood friend. They, along with Balarama, stayed in sage Sandeepani's ashrama. Once Shri Krishna and Balarama went to the forest to fetch firewood. The guru's wife sent Sudama also to the forest. She gave him some grams, to be shared by the three of them in case they felt hungry. When he met Shri Krishna in the forest, Shri Krishna told him that he was thirsty. Sudama replied that it was not good to drink on an empty stomach and to rest for some time. Shri Krishna lay down and put his head on Sudama's lap. When he saw that Shri Krishna was asleep, Sudama began to eat the grams quietly. Shri Krishna heard the sound and asked Sudama what he was eating. Sudama said that there was nothing to eat and his teeth were chattering due to the cold. Shri Krishna said that he had dreamt that someone was eating another person's share and when questioned, answered that there was nothing except dust and then the word 'tathastu' was heard. For the untruthful words spoken by Sudama, he had to suffer from the most extreme poverty until he repaid the Lord by offering the rice which was sent by his wife. When Sudama (Kuchela) brought that humble offering, his mind was pure and full of devotion.

Baba is the incarnation of truth. He was insistent that his devotees should always behave virtuously by maintaining truthfulness and transparency in their words, thoughts, actions and behaviour. There are many incidents in Satcharita which depicts this principle. Baba shunned hypocrisy altogether. People often get prejudiced and overlook the virtues of others. If we cannot agree with another person's behaviour or any other trait, the truthful way is to tell him directly. If we cannot do it, better be silent. A person who is true to his own self will not judge or defame others. A truthful person will be straightforward in all dealings. Baba shunned hypocrisy altogether. There are two incidents where Baba teaches two such people the correct way of behaviour.

Baba Compares a Critic to a Sow

Once a great devotee was prejudiced and criticised another person behind his back. The virtues were overlooked and only negatives traits were recounted. The omniscient Baba knew this. On the way to the Lendi, Baba enquired about that particular devotee and was told that he was at the village stream for toilet purposes. Later, Baba met him on the way. A village sow was eating excreta, next to a hedge. Baba pointed to the sow and told that devotee:

> Look how its tongue is enjoying the taste of human excreta! A person who reviles his own brethren to his heart's content is similar to it.
>
> Chapter 19, verse 205

> If you are born as a human being, after doing a lot of good deeds in your previous birth, and if you thus waste the life, what good can Shirdi do for him who is set to ruin himself?
>
> Chapter 19, verse 206

Baba's words went straight to the devotee's heart. He remembered the morning's incident and was repentant. Criticisms without basis and belittling a person in his absence is definitely falsehood.

Baba Exposes the False Behaviour of a Lawyer

Once a lawyer came to the masjid and had Baba's darshan. He offered dakshina without being asked and sat near Baba. Baba turned towards the lawyer and said:

> What frauds people are! They touch my feet, offer dakshina also and abuse me in the heart-of-heart. How queer are their ways!
>
> Chapter 21, verse 109

This lawyer's munsif had gone to Shirdi and stayed there to be with Baba, because of ill-health. The lawyers in the chamber criticised the munsif's behaviour as superstition and belittled both the munsif and Baba. The lawyer also participated in this back-biting. Baba pointed out his false behaviour. The lawyer realised his mistake and decided to refrain from such undesirable practices in the future. He clearly understood that wherever he might be, whatever he did, would be known to Baba. This is a lesson for all devotees. We should be straightforward and avoid evil company which leads us to commit wrong actions.

Labourers Should Be Paid Duly

Baba did not approve hypocritical behaviour, cheating or accepting free services. It is a common practice of people either to underpay or not to suitably pay the labourers who serve them. People will spend lavishly for their enjoyments, but when it comes to paying a manual labourer or servant, they bargain and become reluctant to pay even small amounts. Baba insisted that everybody's labour should be duly compensated. There is an incident narrated in Satcharita regarding this.

Once Radhakrishnabai suffered from severe malaria and was restless. Baba was also weak at that time. But he suddenly came near Radhakrishnabai's house with some devotees and asked for a ladder. Someone brought a ladder and Baba put it against the wall of the neighbouring house of Waman Gondkar, climbed it and crossed over quickly to Radhakrishnabai's roof. Then he crossed to the other side of the roof. The ladder was shifted to that wall and Baba descended. As soon as Baba came down, he meticulously gave two rupees to the person who had brought the ladder and placed it at two places. When the devotees asked Baba about such a liberal remuneration, he replied:

> Nobody should take another's labour, in any way, free of charge.
>
> Chapter 19, verse 246
>
> One can accept work from a person but one should always evaluate a person's efforts and repay. One should discipline oneself never to take free services from anyone.
>
> Chapter 19, verse 247

The truthful way of accepting a service is to judge properly the efforts involved in a work and duly pay the person who undertook that work. Accepting a service and not paying duly even after knowing the efforts involved is falsehood.

Dada Kelkar's Hypocritical Behaviour

Dada Kelkar was a great devotee of Baba. He strictly followed all religious observances according to his belief system. But compared to the guru's orders, rules of religious observances are of no value. A disciple should faithfully obey the guru's orders even if it means breaking religious norms. Once Baba prepared pulao (with mutton). Baba asked Dada Kelkar whether he had seen how it had turned out. Kelkar casually said that it was very good. Baba told him that he had never seen it with his eyes nor had he tasted it. He asked him to feel it with his own hand and then took his hand himself and thrust it into the pot.

Baba told him, 'Do not care for your orthodoxy. Do not unnecessarily bluster.' A disciple should always obey the orders of guru with utmost sincerity and truthfulness. This is the lesson from this incident.

Appa Kulkarni's Promise

Once Baba visited Appa Kulkarni's house in the guise of a fakir. Appa was not at home at that time as he was away on official duty. His wife offered one rupee to the fakir and thought that she had seen Baba himself. Later Appa had to return home as his horse was not well. When he came to know that the fakir was given only one rupee, he said that if he had been there, he would have given ten rupees. He went out to search for the fakir. But he could not find him. Then he had his lunch and again went to search for the fakir. Soon he found him. The fakir stretched his hand. Appa gave one rupee. But the fakir asked more and Appa gave him three rupees and even borrowed another three rupees from his friend. Since the fakir demanded still more, he took him to his home and gave another three rupees. When the fakir again asked for more money, he told him that he had only one ten-rupee note left with him. The fakir accepted the ten-rupee note, returned the nine coins received earlier and then went away. Appa had earlier said that he would have given ten rupees to the fakir. But when it came to actually giving it, he wavered. By this incident, Baba teaches the lesson that we should be truthful in words and acts. We should fulfil the promises we make. That is why Baba repeatedly asked for money until he received ten rupees. Forgetting the promises is not good.

Balasaheb Deo and Parayana of *Jnaneswari*

Deo had difficulty in initiating regular parayana of *Jnaneswari*. He decided that until Baba instructed him to read it, he would have faith and wait. After some time, he visited Shirdi and had Baba's darshan. He met Jog there. Jog asked him why he was not reading the pothy regularly and even advised him to take a copy and submit it to Baba so that Baba would grace him. Deo rejected Jog's suggestion by saying that Baba knew his inner thoughts and must clearly tell him to read the pothy. Later, he happened to meet Balakram. He became curious to know how Balakram was initiated into spirituality by Baba. He made such enquiries to Balakram. Immediately, he was called to the masjid by Baba. When he reached there, Baba was alone. Baba told him that someone had stolen his rags and asked him to search and find it out. Deo could not understand what Baba meant by 'rags' and he could not find anything. Suddenly, Baba became furious and accused him of stealing the rags. He was frightened and feared that Baba would beat him. Yet at the same time he was amazed also. Baba asked him to go away from there.

Later, Baba called him in the evening and told him to read the pothy. By rags Baba had meant the enquiries made by Deo to Balakram. A disciple should not resort to indirect ways. He should be truthful in his words. Here Deo already decided and even told Jog that unless Baba clearly told him to read the pothy, he would not start reading it. But when he met Balakram he wanted to know how he was initiated and advised by Baba. Baba considered such enquiries as untruthful and improper behaviour. A disciple should completely depend on his guru for any sort of guidance in spiritual practices even if it means waiting for a long period.

Ramadasi's Hypocritical Behaviour

Once a group of devotees belonging to Ramadasi tradition came to Shirdi. Only the leader's wife had genuine devotion and hence Baba gave her darshan as Lord Rama. She told her husband about the darshan. The man ridiculed her and rubbished her words. The same night Baba appeared in his dream. In that vision the man saw himself locked up in a prison in some city. His hands were tied tightly behind him with ropes. He saw Baba standing outside the lock-up, and quietly watching the scene. The man prayed to Baba to save him. Baba told him that one should suffer the consequences of one's deeds. The man said that he had not done anything wrong at least in the present life. Baba replied that then it must have been in another life. The man said that he did not know anything about the previous lives and if anything was there it should be burnt to ashes by Baba's darshan. Baba asked the man if he had so much faith and told him to shut his eyes and the man did the same. Suddenly he heard a loud sound and he opened his eyes. He saw himself free, but the policeman was lying on the floor soaked in blood. Baba told him that officer would come and he would be caught and held responsible for the act. The man was frightened and prayed fervently to Baba to save him from the problem. Baba asked him to shut his eyes again and the man obeyed. When he opened his eyes, he was outside the lock-up and Baba was near him. The man performed an eight-fold obeisance. Baba asked him whether there was any difference between the prostrations made earlier and those made then. He replied that there was a difference as of sky and earth – the earlier prostrations were made for monetary benefits and present prostrations were made to acknowledge him as God. He said that earlier he had no faith in him and thought that Baba was a Muslim and was defiling Hindus. Baba asked him whether he had a panja in his home and if he had not worshipped the tabut. Baba hinted that the man used to worship a Muslim deity called Kada Bibi. The man admitted all these facts. Baba knew his inner thoughts, duplicity and religious hypocrisy. So he exposed it through that vision. After that dream, the man's thinking was changed and his baseless antagonism disappeared.

Conclusion

Truthfulness is the eternal virtue upon which this universe exists. It is the synonym of Paramatman. For devotees of Sai, it is the greatest ornament. It promotes the quality of purity (sattva) and progression in spirituality. In mundane dealings and spiritual life, we should try to be honest and straight in all our dealings. In the present mundane world, which has its existence and sustenance on falsehood, it is extremely difficult to be always truthful in all areas. Such a person will be subjected to many trials and tribulations. But people who have based their life on Baba's teachings will be able to overcome any obstacles because the guru and God always protect those who truthfully serve them and other fellow beings. The motives behind our actions should be honest and pure. It is the mentality with which an action is performed that is counted, not the action itself. A person can become a murderer or a thief even if he does the same only mentally. So devotees should make their thoughts truthful, then the actions also will become truthful.

HUMILITY

We consider him as an avatar since he had all the attributes of one. But he himself always said: I am a slave at the feet of Allah.

Chapter 23, verse 4

He never said 'I am God' but said 'I am a humble servant of God, I always remember God'. He regularly chanted 'God is the owner (Allah Malik)'.

Chapter 23, verse 8

He did not despise anyone nor considered anyone insignificant. For him each and every object was God. He saw pure consciousness in all.

Chapter 23, verse 7

I am the humblest of your servants. I am your debtor. I have come here to have your darshan.

Chapter 10, verse 90

11

HUMILITY

> He did not compare himself to anyone and did not allow anyone to do it also. Humility is the true ornament of one who considers the whole universe filled with God.
>
> Chapter 23, verse 6

Humility is the most required virtue for spiritual progress. Even in mundane life, humility is a desirable quality for smooth interpersonal interactions. We should have humility as a result of our innate purity, not just fake it with superficial behaviour. When there is internal purity, the feeling of 'I' and 'mine' does not arise. Such persons can accept the authority of a qualified person whole-heartedly. They do not belittle anyone who are lesser intelligent or lesser able than them. They can appreciate other people's virtues. They become receptive to other people's views and beliefs.

This does not mean that they accept all views and opinions blindly. They are able to distinguish between the right and wrong, desirable and undesirable. By being humble, they are not projecting themselves and their importance.

All this is naturally possible only in those people in whom the quality of purity (sattva) prevails. People in whom passion (rajas) and ignorance (tamas) prevails, the feelings of 'I' and 'mine' predominate. So, they will be overwhelmed by anger, pride, hate and confusion. Such characteristics are obstacles in the path of spiritual progress.

Baba not only advised his devotees to be humble, but he himself was humility personified. For the love of his devotees, Baba said:

> This is a great favour of yours that I have been able to reach your feet. I am a maggot in your excreta. I consider myself blessed thereby.
>
> Chapter 10, verse 91

What humility on the part of Baba! What height of complete abandonment of ego! He was equally modest too.

There are many instances in Baba's life which shows this exemplary virtue.

The Story of Jawahar Ali

Humility and obedience are the primary qualities a disciple should possess. Baba himself practised this principle. Jawahar Ali was a fakir from Ahmednagar. He went to Rahata to stay with his disciple. Later he started to construct an Idgah near the Veerabhadra temple. He was charged with having defiled Veerabhadra and was driven out of the village. He was a scholar. He knew the Koran sharif like the palm of his hand. He was a sweet-tongued person. He came to Shirdi and stayed at the masjid with Baba. He told Baba, 'Be my disciple.' Hemadpant says:

> The guru was not aware of the accomplishments of the disciple. But the disciple knew the shortcomings of the guru. But he never showed any disrespect and fulfilled the duties of a disciple.
>
> Chapter 5, verse 126

Baba meticulously carried out all the orders given by the guru. After some time Jawahar Ali took Baba to Rahata.

People thought that Jawahar Ali had captured Sai with his own yogic powers. But Baba's attitude was different. He wanted to show to the people how we should behave without pride. People went to Rahata and brought Baba and Jawahar Ali back to Shirdi. Later, Jawahar Ali was defeated by Devidas in a debate regarding scriptures. Jawahar escaped from there and stayed in Vaijapur. He returned after many years and bowed down to Baba. He repented and was purified. The misconception was cleared up that 'I am the guru and Sai is the chela'.

Baba honoured the concept of the teacher and student relationship by practising it himself. Baba let Jawahar Ali cherish his status as a teacher and accepted his own status as a student. Hemadpant says:

> In such matters ingenuity and intelligence are of no use. One who wants to achieve his own good should behave without pride.
>
> Chapter 5, verse 156

> He who has burnt away his bodily pride is the person who alone has used his body for its proper purpose. To achieve the ultimate good, he may then become anybody's follower or disciple.
>
> Chapter 5, verse 158

Nanavalli

Nanavalli was a realised soul who lived in Shirdi and was an ardent devotee. Outwardly his behaviour was very eccentric. Once he came and asked Baba to get up from his gaddi as he wanted to sit there. Baba got up and left his seat. Nanavalli sat where Baba was sitting. After a while he got up, bowed in front of Baba and went away. When Nanavalli asked him to get up, Baba was least affected. He obliged him and moved away. Nanavalli understood that honour or dishonour had the least effect on Baba. A person who does not have ego will not have pride. He will be humble in front of all living creatures.

There are many incidents where many devotees were mentally reformed and became humble at Baba's feet. Because of their preconceived notions and beliefs their minds were prejudiced. Some of them were proud of their intellectual achievements, learning and religious austerities. This excessive pride prevented them from being pure of heart or humble. Baba did not accept them until they got inner transformation and became humble. Baba made them realise that unless they nurture humility, real knowledge cannot be attained. Experiences of some of such people are described in Satcharita.

Siddique Falke

Siddique Falke was a Muslim resident of Kalyan. He came to Shirdi after a pilgrimage to Mecca–Medina. He stayed in the chavadi for nine months. But Baba was not ready to meet him. He was denied entry to the masjid. Falke was dejected. He requested and persuaded Madhavarao to intervene on his behalf. Madhavarao requested Baba to allow Falke to enter the masjid at least once and have his darshan. Baba put forward three conditions and Madhavarao informed them to Falke. Falke humbly accepted every condition. Meanwhile, Baba became angry and came near Falke. Baba said, 'What do you think yourself to be? Are you boasting in front of me?'

> You are giving yourself airs because of your age! Is that the way you recite the Koran? You are vain because you have done the pilgrimage to Mecca. But you do not realise who I am!
>
> Chapter 11, verse 108

Later Baba cooled down and accepted Falke affectionately. Baba wanted him to get rid of his pride and be humble. Siddique Falke learned this lesson and later behaved suitably.

Muley, the Agnihotri Brahmin

Muley was an orthodox Agnihotri Brahmin from Nasik. He came to meet Shriman Buti in Shirdi. Along with others, Muley went to the masjid and took Baba's darshan. He was proud of his knowledge of palmistry, astrology and scriptures. He strictly adhered to his religious rituals. In his mind he thought that Baba was a Muslim, the masjid was impure and he was not obliged to Baba in any manner. He was a disciple of the late Gholap Guru. After returning from the masjid, he sat for his rituals and avoided going to Baba's aarati.

Baba sent Buti to take dakshina from Muley. Muley came to the masjid, stood at a distance and threw flowers on Baba from there. Baba had worn ochre coloured kafni for the evening aarati. Baba gave darshan of Gholap Guru to Muley. Gholap Guru had already attained samadhi. Muley was so amazed that he forgot all differences which were there in his mind. He ran towards Baba's feet and was immersed in a deep, blissful state. He sang Gholap Guru's praises loudly and was overwhelmed with love. When he stood up and opened his eyes, he saw Baba asking for dakshina. Muley's pride about his high caste vanished. His doubting mind became clear. He became humble at Baba's feet and offered whatever dakshina he had.

The omniscient Baba knew that Muley was attached to his guru, but at the same time highly proud of his orthodox ways. So to make him humble, Baba made him realise the oneness of all gurus.

Megha

Megha was an illiterate Brahmin who was serving Sathe. Sathe sent him to Shirdi to serve Baba. Megha was a devotee of Lord Shiva. In the book *Shri Sai Baba* written by Swami Sai Sharan Anand, the author says that when Sathe asked Megha to go to Shirdi, Megha asked, 'What's the caste of your guru?' When he heard that Baba stayed in a masjid and people did not know whether he was a Muslim or a Hindu, he assumed that Baba was Muslim and told Sathe, 'Can a yavana ever be a guru? No, never.' Sathe compelled him a lot and he finally agreed to go to Shirdi.

Even though Megha went to Shirdi, he had no inner conviction. Pride can be of different types – of wealth, status, family, position, caste and so on. Megha had pride in his caste. Baba knew his inner thoughts and so did not allow him to enter the masjid. Baba said to him:

> Beware, if you put your feet on the steps! This place is inhabited by a Muslim.
>
> Chapter 28, verse 138

> You are a high caste Brahmin and I the lowest of the low, a Muslim. You will be defiled. Go back.
>
> Chapter 28 verse 139

Any type of pride is a hindrance to spiritual progress. Baba wanted Megha to shed the caste pride and progress in spirituality.

Megha stayed in Shirdi for a few days and returned home. There he fell sick and was confined to bed. He began to contemplate on Baba wholeheartedly. He came back to Shirdi. He became humble and devoted to Baba.

Baba Asked Dakshina to Teach Humility

When people started to flock to Shirdi, Baba started asking

for dakshina. Baba asked dakshina because of many reasons. Firstly, he could sort out selfless devotees amongst the vast number of those visiting him. Secondly, he wanted to teach his devotees' detachment. Thirdly, he wanted to teach them humility. Some devotees who had pride about their wealth were repeatedly asked for dakshina until they were left with nothing. When they realised the fact that their ability to provide was limited, they became humble.

Humility is the first step for absorbing the teacher's instructions. Sometimes Baba used to send the rich devotees to beg from poor people's homes on his behalf. Even if the person was a millionaire, he would bow his head and obey Baba's order.

Conclusion

Humility is a great virtue. It is necessary for receiving the guru's grace and thus advancement in spiritual progress and self-realisation. By devotion and faith in God and guru, the devotees become purified of passions and ignorance, and the ego will be weakened. Once there is no sense of 'I' and 'mine', they will become humble. It will help them receive God's and guru's full grace. Hemadpant says that scholars are blinded by conceit and are pride personified while a simple, naïve devotee depends on God and guru for crossing the ocean of life.

> The jnani says: There is no God but me for I have attained all knowledge and I am that Pure Consciousness.
> Chapter 32, verse 94

> But a devotee, because of his faith and devotion, does not show off his knowledge. He totally surrenders to the guru and serves his guru with his body, mind and all that he possesses.
> Chapter 32, verse 95

He does not have the conceit to believe that this is the greatness of his prowess or that this is the brilliance of his knowledge.

Chapter 32, verse 96

Leaving all doership to God, he adopts utter humility. A devotee is always dependent upon and he is not independent.

Chapter 32, verse 98

Devotion to God and guru purifies the heart and nurtures humility. May such humility be our only ornament!

COURAGE

Courage is itself patience, oh woman, never let it leave you. In times of difficulties, it will stand you in good stead.
Chapter 19, verse 53

Though a guru is very powerful, he expects only wisdom from his disciple, firm faith, lots of courage and patience at the feet of the guru.
Chapter 19, verse 58

Do not forsake fortitude. Do not let any despondency enter your heart. You will get well. Do not worry. The kind fakir will take care of you.
Chapter 23, verse 53

Go and sit and do not feel disheartened. Let a few days pass. Then we will think further. Do not lose patience and courage.
Chapter 31, verse 36

12

COURAGE

Have a little courage and patience. Pick up the boy carefully. He will regain consciousness.

Chapter 26, verse 77

Courage is the inner firmness and stability in the face of challenging situations or miseries. It is the willingness to undertake a daring, right decision and diligently sticking to its execution in the midst of unfavourable and even harmful circumstances. It is an inner virtue which stems from a sound moral judgement. It is not driven by ego.

In spirituality, the virtue of courage is of paramount importance. Selfless beings, like enlightened masters, are the bravest and the most courageous people in the world. A devotee or a disciple should have the virtue of courage to progress on the path of spirituality. Baba had said that faith, patience and courage are needed to progress in devotion and service to guru and God.

Fearlessness and self-confidence together determine the virtue of courage. Fearlessness and confidence in oneself and the inner conviction of the right path result in courage. A spiritual aspirant should be absolutely fearless in every aspect. Baba assures his devotees of his care so that they remain fearless and stay firm, without any anxieties or worries. Even the gods do the same by showing the hand gesture of fearlessness. Hemadpant says:

That man is independent, he is without fear, he is free and eternal – if this awareness is present, then it can be said that life is fulfilled.

Chapter 8, verse 15

Baba's life itself is an epitome of courage. He chose to live in the undeveloped, remote village of Shirdi. He stayed in a dilapidated masjid among ignorant, poor and illiterate villagers. He executed his mission of spiritual awakening in India and other countries in the midst of all outer constraints – dogmatic views of people belonging to both Hindu and Muslim faiths, ignorant folks whom he had to uplift, baseless criticisms and taunts, communal conflicts and foreign rule. But he laid a concrete foundation for moral living, development of good human qualities, peace, harmony and spiritual growth. This foundation will benefit the humanity for ever. The benefit would be to the whole humanity, irrespective of creed, religion, language or country. Only an incarnation or a godly figure could achieve this task. Baba was extraordinarily courageous. His way of living and instructions are a testimony to this fact.

Hindu–Muslim Harmony

Baba lived in an old masjid. He did not care about outward pomp and show or the approval of people. He loved peace, harmony and moral living. He asked people to stay with their own religious beliefs and guided them to ultimately realise the purpose of human life. He allowed people of all religious beliefs to come to the masjid and perform worship. He allowed the celebration of Rama Navami, Urus, Gokulashtami, Muharram and so on, in the same spirit. He allowed both vegetarian and non-vegetarian food.

He was targeted by the orthodox believers of both religions. But unmindful of all the rivalries, prejudices and dogmatism of the proponents of different religions, Baba achieved his mission. In front of his spiritual aura and its brilliance, their orthodoxy and antagonism disappeared.

Baba did not differentiate between people. Poor and rich, healthy and sick, all were treated equally. He did not have any selfish motives for his life or actions. His life and all actions were for the betterment of humankind. This selflessness and purity generated tremendous courage which adorned all his actions. His entire being was soaked in Supreme Consciousness. He did not care whether people considered him a Hindu or a Muslim. In whatever way people thought, believed and approached him, in the same way he reciprocated. Hemadpant says:

> So long as a person surrendered to God, can he be called a Hindu or Muslim? He may be of a low birth, or low caste, or without a caste. Caste is not the criteria of importance for God.
>
> Chapter 7, verse 19

> One who does not have body consciousness whether he is a Hindu or Muslim, for him all castes and creeds are equal. The discrimination born of caste is not applicable to him.
>
> Chapter 7, verse 20

In a society where people consider religion, caste, family, status and parentage as foremost criteria for assessing a person's worth, Sai Baba lived a whole life only with the titles which were given to him by people. They called him 'Sai', he accepted it; some considered him as a Hindu, others believed he was a Muslim, he did not object; Some considered his residence as a temple and others considered it as a mosque, he allowed both types of rituals to be conducted there. Only an extraordinary incarnation would have such courage to accept and adopt all faiths and guide all people accordingly.

Baba Overturned Villagers' Decision and Purchased Firewood During Cholera Epidemic

On one occasion cholera epidemic spread in Shirdi and the villagers were frightened. As long as the epidemic continued, it was decided not to kill any goat and not to allow any vehicle from outside to enter the village. If anyone broke the regulation, a fine had to be paid before he was let off. Even though there was scarcity of firewood, villagers took this decision.

At that time, a cart from another village, full of firewood, arrived at the village border. The villagers began to send back the cart. Baba came to know about this and went to the spot. He stood before the cart. This gave courage to the cart driver. The obstinacy of the villagers was broken and the cart was allowed inside the village. The firewood was unloaded in front of the masjid. Baba used to store firewood to be burnt in his dhuni. It takes large amount of courage to oppose and overcome the dogmatism of a whole village population. Hemadpant says:

> Baba had no fear of the fine. He was always and at all times fearless. He was merged in God and was victorious over death.
>
> Chapter 23, verse 78

Baba kept his dhuni lighted day and night, continuously. He used to store firewood in the masjid. Many villagers used to request and take firewood for cooking purposes. If we analyse scientifically, we can understand that Baba's action of breaking the rule was apt. Cholera disease is caused by a micro-organism (Vibrio cholera) and it is spread by unhygienic living conditions like water contaminated with faecal matter and contaminated food items (through flies). This micro-organism can be destroyed by boiling water. Also, it is proved that there is no need for isolating the patient or imposing quarantine measures. Good sanitation and hygienic practices are the effective methods. If enough firewood was readily available, the villagers could do proper cooking of food items and boiling of water. Also, firewood could be used by them for cremation of corpses.

Baba's way of living also exemplifies perfect inner courage. He won over his senses and demands of body and mind. He was even-minded in poverty and richness. He did not have a home, relatives or belongings. He performed his mission of uplifting his devotees with equanimity. He wanted his devotees also to be fearless and courageous. A devotee may have to face many calamities and difficulties in both material and spiritual life. We must be able to endure all sufferings and march forward in life. In material life, setbacks in employment and financial crises occur and people find it very difficult to cope with such situations. In extreme desperation, they may even commit suicide. When a devotee was in such a situation, Baba averted his death and gave courage and encouragement through the agency of another devotee and a book.

Averting Ambedkar's Suicide Attempt

Gopal Narayan Ambedkar from Pune was a great devotee of Baba. He lost his job and could not succeed in his independent trading business. His household conditions became unbearable. Utterly disgusted with life, he came to Shirdi and decided to commit suicide. He decided to end his life by jumping into a well. At the same moment the owner of the nearby hotel, Sagun Naik, came out and gave him a copy of the biography of Akkalkot Maharaj. Ambedkar turned the pages and found a story which was similar to his condition. When a devotee who was suffering from a long-standing illness decided to commit suicide and jumped into a well, Akkalkot Maharaj came there, pulled him out with his own hands and advised him, 'Whatever is destined has to be fully borne.'

If this suffering remains unfinished, you have to be born again. Therefore, try to bear up with this trouble a little longer. Do not kill yourself.

Chapter 26, verse 139

Baba inspired Sagun and made the book an instrument to divert Ambedkar's mind from committing suicide. Through the words of Akkalkot Maharaj, Baba instilled courage in him to face the ordained sufferings and act with equanimity. Ambedkar worked hard and his adverse circumstances changed. He became happy in his life. His family prospered as he became well-versed in astrology by his own effort.

Baba Advised His Devotees to Be Courageous and Keep Faith in Adverse Circumstances

Bodily ailments, illnesses and accidents, all torment humans in their life. Ordinarily, during such periods, most people become grief-stricken, dejected and desperate. They fear the worst and even wait for death. In the chapter 'Faith' we saw how devotees kept unflinching faith in Baba and fully depended on his words for cure of diseases and other afflictions. On those occasions, Baba advised them to be courageous and patient. Baba's miraculous power was the curative in those occasions. Still, Baba gave them the advice of courage. By such advice, Baba was giving a very practical instruction. Modern medicine has confirmed that when a person is fearful, the immune system in his body malfunction. The endocrine glands secrete stress hormones which, in turn, weaken the body's disease-fighting capacity. But once there is no fear, the immune system and hormones work harmoniously. This accelerates healing and recovery. Since there is a strong interrelationship between body and mind, a fearful state of the mind can affect the health of the body. It will also affect mental functions like clarity, decisiveness and judgement.

In the chapter 'Faith', we saw that Shama solely depended on Baba. He had unflinching faith in Baba. At that time Baba told him:

> Do not forsake fortitude. Do not let any despondency enter your heart. You will get well. Do not worry. The kind Fakir will take care of you.
>
> Chapter 23, verse 53
>
> Go home and sit quietly. Do not go out of the house. Be fearless and free from anxiety. Have faith in me.
>
> Chapter 23, verse 54

By these words Baba was instilling courage in him. It was Baba's miraculous power that saved Shama from untimely death. But Baba was giving the lesson that along with faith, we should also have courage to receive his grace.

Some people believe in astrology, horoscope and prophesies. If they predict happy news, they rejoice. If they predict mishaps, they get dejected and sad. Once, Buti was in Shirdi and at that time Nana Dengle, who was a famous astrologer, predicted that some calamity would fall upon Buti. After hearing the prediction, Buti became restless. He kept worrying all the time. When the group went to the masjid and sat with Baba, Baba asked Buti:

> Well what does this Nana say? Does he predict your death? You have nothing to fear. Retort to him without any hesitation, 'You can kill me if you dare to!'
>
> Chapter 22, verse 97, 98

In the evening Buti went outside to the toilet. At that time a snake came there. Seeing that terrible creature, he ran out. His servant thought of killing the snake and tried to pick up a stone. But Buti stopped him and told to bring a stick instead. When the servant went to bring the stick, the snake escaped.

It was Baba's grace that saved him that day. We should imbibe the lesson which Baba wanted us to learn – that we should be courageous and ready to face any situation. Buti had been restless and anxious on hearing the prediction of the astrologer, but Baba's words gave him courage. So when he had to face the encounter with the snake, he could act with presence of mind.

When a son or a daughter becomes ill or is about to die, the worry and grief of parents cannot be described. At such times, they suffer more mental agony than if they themselves were ill. They become devastated and feel helpless.

In Satcharita, in chapter 26, there is a story about Harish Chandra Pitale's son, who suffered from epilepsy. No treatment was of any benefit. So Pitale brought his son for Baba's darshan. As soon as the boy's eyes met Sai's, the boy became unconscious and fell down. He had a severe attack of fits. The parents became frantically worried. The mother started crying. Baba assured them, 'Have a little courage and patience. Pick up the boy carefully. He will regain consciousness.'

As per Baba's instructions they took the boy to their lodgings and soon the boy recovered.

In this incident, the parents had come to Baba with hope and faith in him. But when the boy had a severe attack and he fell down lifeless, the parents were devastated. Baba advised them to be courageous and patient. Thus, they were able to take the boy to their lodgings and by Baba's grace, the boy recovered.

Baba's Advice to Spiritual Aspirants

Courage is essential for spiritual progress. Baba advised the old lady who was very keen to obtain a mantra from him that courage wards off the sins, worries and miseries. The difficulties are cleared and fear and panic vanish. He further said that although a guru is very powerful, he expects wisdom and lots of courage from the disciple. Along with that the disciple should maintain faith and patience. The virtue of courage helps the aspirant to stick to his goal in the midst of turmoil of material life. Courage helps an aspirant to persist in his spiritual practices even if there won't be any apparent progress. The aspirant should not be disheartened even if he does not get any explicit directions from the guru or he cannot stay in guru's presence.

Even for advanced aspirants the quality of courage is essential. In the chapter on 'Attachment' we saw how Baba had advised the ascetic Vijayananda who was worried about his mother's illness. At that time Baba knew that the ascetic's own end was near. Baba told him to be courageous as there were thieves in the wada, that is, the ascetic's own end was near. Baba told him:

> Go and sit and do not feel disheartened. Let a few days pass. Then we will think further. Do not lose patience and courage.
>
> Chapter 31, verse 36

Baba's words instilled fearlessness and firmness in the ascetic and he was able to do parayana of *Bhagavatapuranam*. A spiritual aspirant should essentially be courageous so that he is not overwhelmed by grief and sorrow. Baba's advice is very relevant even for common people. Baba gives us the lesson that even in the midst of extremely sorrowful situations, we should be courageous so that we can analyse the situation properly and find solutions. We have heard many incidents where people died of accidents and cardiac arrest after hearing the news of death of their relatives. This happens because of sorrow and fear. But if a person has the quality of courage, he will not plunge into sorrow and become fearful or uncertain.

Conclusion

The virtue of courage is of paramount importance in mundane as well as spiritual life. It is the inner firmness and stability in the face of challenging situations or miseries. A devotee or seeker should cultivate the quality of courage so that he will be able to overcome all types of setbacks and keep faith in God and the guru. Courage sustains faith and enlivens patience. Thus, it enables the devotee to receive the grace of God and the guru.

CHANTING OF GOD'S NAME

For the purification of the inner self, there is no other simpler means than chanting the Lord's name. The Lord's name is the adornment of the tongue. The Lord's name sustains spirituality.

        Chapter 27, verse 88

It is not necessary to have a bath to say the Lord's name. Taking the Lord's name is not regulated by the rules of the sastras. The Lord's name destroys all sins. The Lord's name is always pure.

        Chapter 27, verse 89

The continuous chanting of my name itself will ferry you across the ocean of existence. No other means are necessary to achieve salvation.

        Chapter 27, verse 90

Whoever frequently repeats my name, his sins will be burnt. I consider him more virtuous than the virtuous, who constantly hums my name.

        Chapter 27, verse 91

Blessed is the greatness of chanting of Lord's name! Even the guru then remembers the devotee. The meditator becomes the meditated upon, both completely forgetting themselves.

        Chapter 37, verse 92

13

CHANTING OF GOD'S NAME
Naamajapa

Baba loved naama-smarana. He himself constantly repeated the words 'Allah Malik'. He would arrange for a seven-day ceaseless chanting of the naama in his presence, day and night.

Chapter 4, verse 82

Remembering God's form and chanting God's name is one of the ways of practising devotion (navavidha bhakti). Material life happens because of ignorance. Material life revolves around passions, desires and delusions. Devotion to God and guru dispels ignorance and imparts dispassion and divine knowledge. The human form is the best instrument for achieving self-realisation, provided we resort to the right means and ways.

The great Saint Samartha Ramadas says in his holy text *Dasabodha* that human life should be used wisely for achieving self-realisation. He says that the time for everyone is less and therefore without wasting a single moment we should submit to God, pray to him and worship him. By worshipping God, we attain dispassion and divine knowledge.

Baba advised navavidha bhakti to worship God. Chanting God's name and remembering God's form is a very easy method to practice devotion. God is highly pleased with this simple method of worship. The greatest sinner of yore the Brahmin Ajamila, at the time of his death, called his youngest child with much affection and love – Narayana. Since this is one of the thousand names of Lord Vishnu, the servitors of Lord Vishnu rushed to snatch the life of Ajamila from the hands of the servants of Lord Yama. Thus, such a grave sinner was redeemed only because he uttered the Lord's name with intense affection and love, even though he did it without conscious intention. Then, what is not possible to achieve by chanting the name with full attention and intention?

Citing the example of Ajamila, if someone thinks that he can wait till the last hour, there is no guarantee that he will remember God's name at that hour. So, the most practical course of action is to remember and chant the Lord's name always and install his image in our heart at all times and fully surrender to that Supreme Power.

Hemadpant says:

> In kritayuga it was controlling the senses and subduing of passions, in tretayuga sacrifices, in dwaparayuga rituals and in kaliyuga reciting the name and singing the praises – a simple means of salvation.
>
> Chapter 3, verse 53

Significance of Chanting of God's Name

Baba loved God's name and he himself always chanted 'Allah Malik' (God is the master). He gave *Vishnusahasranama* to Madhavarao (Shama) and advised him to recite it. Baba explained to him about the greatness of name chanting as follows:

> God's name can break down mountains of sin. The Lord's name breaks the shackles of the body. God's name pulls out crores of ill desires from their roots.
>
> Chapter 27, verse 85

God's name humbles the pride of death and ends the cycle of birth and death. I want Shama to be interested in this treasure of *Sahasranama*.

Chapter 27, verse 86

The Lord's name chanted with full interest is very effective but even an unintentional pronouncement can be beneficial. Its power is manifested even when it is uttered unawares.

Chapter 27, verse 87

The reading and study of *Sahasranama* is a general way of purifying the mind and is of ancient origin. That is why Baba asked Shama to recite it.

The Lord's name can be chanted at anytime, anywhere. It does not need any pre-requisites like bath, etc. It can be chanted even while doing any mundane activity.

Baba loved the naamajapa and used to arrange for a seven-day ceaseless chanting of naama. Once Baba asked Das Ganu to conduct such a seven-day chanting and at the end of the seventh day Das Ganu had darshan of Lord Vittal.

There are many incidents described by Hemadpant where Baba advised and encouraged chanting. Some of such incidents are given here.

Rohilla's Story

Once a Rohilla – a Muslim Pathan – came to Shirdi and became devoted to Baba. He was hefty and huge. He was self-willed and cared for no one. Sitting in the masjid, he used to recite the verses from Koran very loudly, with extreme enthusiasm. He did not care whether his voice was loud and shrill. Nature had endowed him with a rattling voice. Whenever he felt inspired, he would start shouting the name of God. He continued this day and night.

Baba was not troubled by the loud chanting. But the villagers, who had to work during day in the fields and forests, were disturbed in their sleep. They felt tired due to lack of sleep. This became a nuisance for them. The Rohilla became uncontrollable as he had Baba's support and he continued to shout loudly all the time. So, the villagers complained to Baba so that he would stop the nuisance. Baba told them not to interfere with the Rohilla as his shouts would drive away his evil qualities. All this shouting was helpful for him (Baba) also. Baba told the villagers that when the Rohilla got tired, he would keep quiet on his own. People were amazed at Baba's forbearance. Hemadpant says:

> Baba disliked association with one who loathed God's name. Then why would he think of driving away the Rohilla, when he was continuously repeating God's name?
>
> Chapter 3, verse 139

> In this manner Baba conveyed the lesson to one and all that he liked the Rohilla's company because he loved God's name.
>
> Chapter 3, verse 140

> The things perceived, one who perceives and that which he perceives (all the three) is God for him. Such a person, whether he be a Brahmin or a Pathan, is regarded as the same.
>
> Chapter 3, verse 141

Hemadpant and Ram Naama

Once while he was in Shirdi, on a Wednesday night, Hemadpant fixed his mind on chanting the name of Ram next day, that is, Thursday. In the morning, when he woke up, he was reminded of the name of Ram. So his decision was reinforced. After his morning ablutions he went to have Baba's darshan. When he reached near the masjid, he heard Aurangabadkar singing a song about Lord Ram, carrying a tamburi in his hand, facing Baba, in the courtyard. The meaning of the song was 'The disciple of Janardhan was seeing only Ram within him, without him, in sleep, in dream and everywhere.' Aurangbadkar knew many songs, but he was inspired to sing this particular song at that time. Hemadpant realised that Baba was encouraging him to stay with his resolve.

Hemadpant describes the greatness of Ram Naama. The bandit fisherman was turned into Sage Valmiki by the power of the word. He recited 'mara, mara'. The words got merged and they became 'Ram, Ram'.

> The name of Ram is the most pious, by which the sinner can be salvaged. The name of Ram brings treasures of joy. The name of Ram is equivalent to singing bhajans and its recitation can lead to Brahman.
>
> Chapter 19, verse 184

> By simple repeated utterance of the name of Ram, the bonds of birth and death will be broken. By the remembrance of the name of Ram the gains will be multifold.
>
> Chapter 19, verse 185

> Whenever the name of Ram resounds, the Sudarshana Chakra of Vishnu will operate and it will destroy millions of obstacles. The name is the protector of the weak.
>
> Chapter 19, verse 186

Mrs Khaparde

A highly learned and knowledgeable person, who had English education, Mr Khaparde once came to Shirdi and stayed there for four months. He was well known in the Council of State and was a good orator. His wife was very devout and had immense love for Baba. She stayed in Shirdi for seven months. Once, while relishing the naivedya prepared by her, Baba spoke about her previous lives. Pleased by her devotion and service, Baba told her to keep on repeating 'Rajaram, Rajaram'. Baba said:

> Keep chanting this always. Oh, mother, your life's objective will be achieved, your mind will be at peace, and you will be immensely benefitted.
>
> Chapter 27, verse 167

These words penetrated her heart and stayed there. Hemadpant says that through those words Baba had instantly imparted shaktipath. When the guru advises to repeat a particular word or mantra, it contains tremendous power.

The greatness of naamajapa is huge. It has no limitations. It can be practised anywhere and at any time. Ideally, the naama should be chanted always, in all circumstances, whether one is happy or unhappy. Even the illiterates and fools have benefitted from it. We should chant the Lord's name all the time we are awake. If that is not possible, it should be done at least in the morning, afternoon and evening.

When Goddess Parvati asked Lord Siva about a simple method by which people can get benefit of chanting *Vishnusahasranama*, the Lord replied that one Ram naama is equal to a thousand names. Samartha Ramadas says that Lord Siva could digest the strongest poison, because of constant chanting of Ram naama. Even in recent times, many people have benefitted materially and spiritually by the practice of naamajapa. Many people received enlightenment and also cure of physical maladies. Pujya Shri Mota (Chunilal Ashram Bhavsar, Hari Om Foundation, Surat) described in his autobiography how he was cured of epilepsy by continuous name chanting. Mata Anandamayidevi and Shri Ramadas of Anand ashram had also expounded the greatness of Lord's name by citing their own life.

Conclusion

In this world all things are God (Brahman) including sound, speech, sight and so on. A name represents the person and his form. God's name is God's form and essence. Constant chanting with faith and devotion will break the shackles of illusion and lead us to liberation. By continuous chanting of God's name, those who are immersed in various troubles of family life will have a constant awareness of the divinity. It will give relief for the innumerable problems of material life and provide a divine armour against troubles. In the end, it will take us to liberation.

> When one is unfailingly involved in singing the Lord's name, the sins, sufferings and poverty disappear. The Lord runs and helps him who meditates on him with love and affection.
>
> Chapter 31, verse 44

STUDY OF HOLY TEXTS

Then Baba ordered: 'Let there be more recitation. By reading this *Gurucharitra* devotees are purified.'

Chapter 18, verse 56

If this book is recited repeatedly, it will be beneficial for them. They will receive God's blessings and the worldly chains will be broken off.

Chapter 18, verse 57

'Ritual' means to read a certain portion regularly. If not fully understood or done half-way, one should not get up and leave it unfinished. Otherwise upasana is incomplete.

Chapter 18, verse 79

Listening to this Satcharita or reciting it regularly will result in the feet of Sai Samartha removing all the difficulties without any delay.

Chapter 52, verse 47

Reading the book with reverence, Sai Samarth is propitiated. He destroys ignorance and poverty and grants knowledge and untold prosperity.

Chapter 52, verse 49

14

STUDY OF HOLY TEXTS

> Sloth, wandering of mind, attachment to sense objects and indulgence of the palate – these are the obstacles which come in the way of listening. Steer clear of these and the listening will become a happy experience.
>
> Chapter 3, verse 181

Religious texts or scriptures and company of realised masters help us to cross the mundane life and reach the shore of self-realisation. Religious texts are representatives of inner experience of realised sages, saints, masters and prophets. As a result of their intense meditation and contemplation, they were able to get direct communion with Paramatman. They conveyed their inner experience and the philosophical truths that derived from it to their disciples and followers.

In ancient times this was passed through oral tradition. Later, it was preserved in palm leaves and then on paper. The religious texts are meant for humans to evolve from base nature to higher states and realise the goal of human life, that is, to be in union with the ultimate truth. The enlightened masters knew that the human mind has an avid affinity for visible forms. Its basic nature and essential need is love. Except for a few, most people cannot grasp, retain or contemplate the ultimate truth as pure consciousness, which is formless and is devoid of any property. So the masters emphasised the path of devotion. They praised the ultimate truth in visible forms. The omniscient, omnipresent, omnipotent pure consciousness can assume the form which is being contemplated by devotees.

The masters propitiated gods and goddesses through devotional hymns, songs and stories. Since stories can have strong impact on human minds, Puranas were created. Along with stories, philosophical truths regarding the Paramatman were also passed on. By listening to and reading of religious texts, people could progress on the path of devotion and gain wisdom, peace of mind and love for the chosen deities. In the course of time, devotion leads to the realisation of the formless nature of Paramatman and self-realisation.

Only the literature describing the prowess of the Paramatman is worth listening. The practices of writing and listening about human activities and mundane lives are neither conducive to inner growth nor provide mental peace. The sage Vyasa divided Vedas and rearranged them so that humans of Kaliyuga would be able to grasp at least some part of them. He created the Puranas and the great epic Mahabharata. But still his mind was not at peace. It was ever restless. Then as per sage Narada's advice, he wrote *Bhagavatapuranam*, which depicts the life and leelas of Lord Shri Krishna. Then his mind became peaceful. Even now, by reading *Bhagavatapuranam*, anybody's mind will become still, tranquil and detached.

Acquiring knowledge through intellectual exercises will not help in developing love for Paramatman. It will not make the mind steady or calm. Look at the example of Anantrao Patankar who had memorised all the shastras, Upanishads, Vedas and Vedangas. He came and surrendered at Baba's feet, requesting him to show the path by which his mind would experience peace and tranquillity. Baba advised him to practise navavidha bhakti.

Study of Holy Texts

Reading and studying holy texts is very important for developing devotion, wisdom and detachment. The texts are like trusted companions. The time spent in reading holy texts and being in the company of saints is the only time which can be considered well utilised. Baba encouraged his devotees to read, listen and contemplate on their respective religious texts. Once the guru blesses, the study of texts becomes easier and the content and inner meaning will be well understood.

Baba encouraged the devotees to read life stories and teachings of saints. In Satcharita, Hemadpant has described how Baba advised and helped devotees to read and contemplate on religious texts. Baba advised how to do parayana and to get benefitted from it, and also about which things that should be avoided to have effective reading.

> One who is desirous of obtaining knowledge should listen so intently that he becomes one with the preaching, with assimilation. Thus the Supreme Energy will appear before him and the mind will be elevated.
>
> Chapter 3, verse 151

> Even if one is engrossed in worldly affairs and one chances to hear the tales of a saint, without making the slightest efforts, they will still do good because such is their nature.
>
> Chapter 3, verse 152

> The devotion to the guru's feet will develop and the well-being will tremendously increase gradually. No other rites or rituals are necessary. The supreme good will be attained.
>
> Chapter 3, verse 154

Once the mind is disciplined in this way the longing to listen to the stories will increase. The bonds of sense objects will easily break away and extreme happiness will pervade.

Chapter 3, verse 155

Baba's Advice to an Assistant Collector Regarding Reading

Once a certain gentleman, who had the privilege of an education in English, became an Assistant Collector. During the earlier period of his career, he was a clerk in a government office. While he was camping in Vadegaon, he went for having darshan of a holy person. The holy person advised him to read *Vicharasagara* of Saint Nischal Das. The holy person told him that later he would travel to North and meet a saint and that saint would guide him further.

The work in Vadagaon was completed and he was transferred to Junnar. On the way to Junnar, he had to cross Nane Ghat. He had to traverse the steep hill on the back of a male buffalo and had to suffer much trouble. Later, he came to Shirdi to have Baba's darshan. Baba told him:

> The path of this place is not as easy as the teachings of the Kanares Appa or even as the buffalo ride in the ghats. There is no alternative but to put in your best exertions.

Chapter 21, verse 62

Whatever Appa has told you is correct. But when you put it into practice, then only will your wishes be fulfilled.

Chapter 21, verse 69

Study of Holy Texts

> First you must read the book carefully, then ponder upon it. With repeated readings, it will lead to total absorption in the subject.
>
> Chapter 21, verse 71
>
> Just reading is not enough. It should be put into practice. otherwise it is like water on a duck's back.
>
> Chapter 21, verse 72
>
> Mere reading is a waste of time till the meaning is not experienced, for which the blessings of a guru, who has the knowledge of the Brahman is required. Mere bookish knowledge is futile.
>
> Chapter 21, verse 73

From this it is evident that the devotees' or aspirants' self-efforts and practise coupled with complete faith in guru and the guru's blessings are needed for realising the meaning and purport of any religious texts.

Baba instructed and directed many devotees to read and make discourses on religious texts. In Shirdi, devotees used to bring religious texts and offered them to Baba. Baba would return the book with his blessings. Sometimes he would not return the books to the original owner and instead he would give to Shama and ask him to keep them and maintain them well by covering them with cloth. Hemadpant says that Baba did this for the benefit of devotees who would come and gather in Shirdi. They could utilise the books and can have mutual discussions. This was also an indication to encourage the reading of religious books.

Religious Texts Read by Devotees in Shirdi

Hemadpant has mentioned some of the religious texts that devotees used to read and hold discourses in Shirdi.

1. **Shri Gurucharitra:** This is the life-story and teachings of Lord Dattatreya and his incarnations Shripada Shrivallabha and Shri Narasimhasaraswathi. Baba had high regards for *Shri Gurucharitra*. Hemadpant has described how Baba graced Sathe when he completed one parayana of *Gurucharitra* by appearing in his dream. Later Dikshit requested Baba to explain the purpose of the vision and asked whether Sathe should do more reading or what he had done was enough. Baba asked him to do one more parayana of the text. Baba told him that by repeated reading of that book, the devotees would get God's blessings and the worldly chains would be broken.

2. **Jnaneswari:** This is a commentary on Bhagavat Gita, written by the saint Shri Jnaneswar. It is also called *Bhavartha Deepika*. Baba made his devotees read this text, together with *Natha Bhagavatam*. Baba commissioned Sakharam Hari Jog to read it at Sathe's wada and the devotees gathered there were benefitted. Every afternoon, after the meals, Jog would go to Baba, bow down at his feet, receive Udi from Baba and ask for permission to start the reading of the pothy. Baba would direct devotees to go and listen to the reading. Sometimes Baba would tell stories in brief. When the devotes listened to the reading, there would be a story by which the meaning of the earlier story told by Baba would be confirmed. The words of the pothy would be similar to those used by Baba in his story. Sometimes Jog would read out some story from the pothy at random, without planning, and it would refer to Baba's story as if by some coincidence.

Once Baba graced Deo and he could read *Jnaneswari* regularly. Later, after few months, Baba appeared in his dream to find out whether he was following the practice regularly.

3. ***Natha Bhagavatam***: This is the commentary for the eleventh skanda of *Bhagavatam*. It is written by Saint Eknath. Baba encouraged devotees to listen to its parayana and also to read it by themselves. In chapter 18 of Satcharita Hemadpant describes an incident where he had been reminded to complete his daily ritual of reading of *Natha Bhagavatam*. He had omitted to do so due to sheer laziness. When Dikshit told Baba about Sathe's dream vision and asked him about its meaning, Baba replied to him that the *Shri Gurucharitra* should be read again. Hemadpant felt that Sathe was graced within seven days and he, who had been reading the same text for seven years was neglected. Baba told him to go to Shama's house and bring dakshina from him, sit and talk with him. When he reached Shama's house, Shama had just finished his bath and started doing pooja. Hemadpant saw the text *Natha Bhagavatam* on the window-sill. He opened it at random and, strangely, it was the same page which he had started to read in the morning but had left incomplete due to laziness. Baba had reminded him to stick to his ritual.

4. ***Vishnusahasranama***: Baba highly revered this holy book. Once he forcefully gave it to Shama, to put him into some regular practice and to give him some prasad of the path of devotion, so that he would get relief from the worldly life. Baba told him that once when He was in distress, he hugged it and held it close to his heart. He felt relief immediately. It seemed as if the Paramatman himself had come down and his life was saved. He told Shama:

Therefore Shama, take it with you. Read it gradually. Every day, take one or two words. It will give you great joy.

Chapter 27, verse 77

Baba advised some other devotees also to study and memorise *Vishnusahasranama*.

5. **Bhagavat Gita**: Baba advised the devotees to read and meditate on the teachings of Gita. He once explained the meaning of chapter IV, verse 34 to Nana Chandorkar. He advised Tilak's commentary on Gita – *Gitarahasya* – to some of the devotees. Once, Jog received a copy of this book and went to the masjid. While prostrating in front of Baba, the parcel fell down and Baba enquired about it. Jog placed it at Baba's feet. Baba took the book out from the parcel, held it in his hand and turned some pages. He took one rupee from his pocket and placed it on the book, with admiration. He handed back the book along with the rupee to Jog and said:

Read it from the beginning to end. You will be benefitted.

Chapter 27, verse 137

6. **Ramayanam**: Baba advised his devotees to read *Adhyatma Ramayanam* and Saint Eknath's *Bhavartha Ramayanam*. By Baba's grace and blessings, Dixit used to read them to other devotees in the wada.

7. **Bhagavatam**: Baba advised the ascetic Vijayanand to complete three readings of *Bhagavatam*. Dixit and other devotees also used to read *Bhagavatam*. Dixit continued this reading during his entire life.

8. **Harivijaya**: Baba also advised reading this book.

Guru's Life Story and Teachings

Reading and listening to the guru's life-story and teachings, and meditation and contemplation on them is the greatest sadhana for devotees and disciples. They should read the life-story and teachings with utmost devotion. The recitation can be completed within a few days or in a few weeks, ritualistically. The procedure for ritualistic reading is described in chapter 52 of Satcharita (as done for *Gurucharitra*). By recitation of the guru's story, Lord Narayana also will be gratified. Hemadpant says:

> One should make it a practice to read at least one chapter of this Satcharita every day, with a calm and concentrated mind. It will bring immediate joy and happiness.
>
> Chapter 52, verse 51
>
> One who desires one's own welfare should really read this book. He will be obliged by Sai, through all the cycles of life and he will remember Sai with overwhelming joy in birth after birth.
>
> Chapter 52, verse 52

Conclusion

Devotees should develop the habit of reading and studying holy texts and the guru's life-story. This helps to cultivate devotion and faith. The religious texts are like a trusted companion. Recitation and study of the guru's life story is the most purifying and beneficial ritual. Devotees should try to avoid distracting factors like sloth, laziness and cravings for pleasures. Ritualistic reading and listening of Satcharita will bestow immense benefits on devotees. It makes devotees pure of heart and will help them to meditate on God and guru. Meditation on God and guru is superior to any knowledge.

COMPANY OF SAINTS

Just as a wick soaked in oil when joined to a flame of light, becomes itself a bright light, in the same way a person reaches the status of a sage at the feet of the sage.

Chapter 3, verse 100

Even casual words uttered by saints break the bonds of false knowledge and save us in times of calamities. So let us assimilate these stories.

Chapter 3, verse 171

To expiate the deadly sins, people take recourse to the water of the Ganga. But Ganga herself resorts to the feet of the saints for washing away her own sins.

Chapter 4, verse 108

If you listen to my stories, recite them and meditate upon them, devotion for me will arise and ignorance will be completely destroyed.

Chapter 2, verse 82

Always do satsang. All other means have some faults. Only satsang is flawless. It is pure in every way.

Chapter 10, verse 142

15

COMPANY OF SAINTS

> Satsang destroys the bodily attachments, such is the power of its strength. Once there is firm faith in it, there is truly liberation from the mundane world.
>
> Chapter 10, verse 143

Satsang means company of holy and virtuous people. The regular company of holy people is rare in the world. It is obtained by God's grace and one's good fortune. Due to meritorious deeds of many past lives, one gets attached to holy persons.

We all know that we are influenced by the company we keep. If we keep good company, we will acquire good qualities and if the company is bad, we will acquire bad qualities. Not only human interactions, but any type of sensual perceptions can influence us – reading, hearing, eating, touching and so on. If we direct our senses to the most desirable outcome, that is, self-realisation, our life will be a blessed one. Otherwise, we can wander in the swamp of material existence and get caught in the never-ending cycle of births and deaths.

Sage Valmiki was originally a hunter who was engaged in robbery and other evil activities to support his family and himself. Once he had an encounter with the seven sages and that changed his destiny. By repeating the word 'mara' continuously, he was transformed into a sage. He became famous as 'Adikavi' and his epic poem Ramayana is known as Adikavyam.

Sage Narada is yet another example of how holy company transforms a person's entire being. In his previous life, sage Narada was the only son of a maidservant. She used to serve in the ashrama of some holy persons. The holy association made a great impression on the mind of the small boy. He developed deep devotion to Lord Narayana. After some time, his mother died of snake bite. Devoid of any bonds to bind him, the boy went on a pilgrimage, longing only for the Lord's vision. Lord Vishnu manifested in his heart and blessed him. In his next life he was born as the mind-son of Lord Brahma and fully devoted to the Lord, singing about his prowess continuously throughout the entire world. That is the magnificent effect of holy company!

In Satcharita, Hemadpant lauds his association with Baba:

> Thanks to the good fortune of the previous births, I have been able to attain his feet, get peace of mind and contentment in household matters.
>
> Chapter 7, verse 26

> Afterwards however much I may prosper, that happiness will never be regained which I experienced and was blessed to receive in the company of the great Shri Sai.
>
> Chapter 7, verse 27

> Sai is the store of ultimate happiness! How could I describe his uniqueness? Whoever surrendered to him was permanently settled for good.
>
> Chapter 7, verse 28

When he came to Shirdi for the first time and had Baba's darshan, the unique experience he felt is described in chapter 2 of Satcharita.

I had never heard of nor seen such a personality. I experienced the gratification of seeing a much-revered person. I lost my hunger and thirst. My senses stood still.

Chapter 2, verse 139

The sins accumulated from many past lives were destroyed by the benevolent glance. Hope awakened of unending joy being received at Sai's feet.

Chapter 2, verse 146

By my good fortune I reached Sai's feet which are as holy as the Lake Manas, which will transform a crow like me into a swan. Sai is a great mahant, foremost amongst saints, ascetic of highest order and a great yogi.

Chapter 2, verse 147

He is the destroyer of sins, difficulties and miseries. By the darshan of such a person as Sai, I am greatly blessed, by coming into contact with the treasure-house of virtue.

Chapter 2, verse 148

Greatness of Saints' Darshan
Saints are God's human forms. They are peace and truth incarnate. Even their merciful glances can burn the heaps of sins accumulated by a person over many past lives. They are personifications of compassion, kindness and purity. Their company gives solace to those who are burnt by the fire of material existence. They act as boats which carry the devotees across the ocean of mundane existence and take them to the abode of the Paramatman. They selflessly strive for the upliftment of humanity. They take birth to impart religiosity and morality. Their teachings help humankind

to rise above animal characteristics and seek the real goal of human life. They look at virtuous and sinful people with equal love. In contrast to gods, they shower their blessings even if unasked and unsought. Gods are pleased only by repeated prayers and surrender. They protect the virtuous by punishing the wicked. But for a saint both types are equal. They will even help the wicked first, to shed their evil ways. Gods can bestow whatever is asked and, at the most, take one to their abode or give their own status. But they cannot make a person as the same as themselves. But a person who is fortunate to get a saint's company shall be transformed into a saint himself. That is why saints are called 'paras' (philosopher's stone) and 'Manas lake'. Paras changes an iron rod into gold and Manas lake transforms an ugly crow into a beautiful swan. Hemadpant further extols the greatness of saints and satsang as follows:

> It is rare to find a person who practises forgiveness, peace, non-attachment, kindness and oblige others, who is in control of his senses and who is devoid of ego.
>
> Chapter 8, verse 85
>
> That which is not achieved through reading books is achieved easily by observing the person who practises all virtues prescribed by the shastras. The sun alone can achieve that which the infinite stars cannot do.
>
> Chapter 8, verse 86
>
> Similar are the noble saints, their numerous simple actions free those who are tied to the world and are a source of extreme pleasure.
>
> Chapter 8, verse 87

If one is fortunate in having satsang, then one understands the preaching easily. At that very moment desire for bad company will melt away. The mind will be free to enjoy the satsang.

Chapter 10, verse 144

In order to attain final emancipation, the only remedy is to have detachment of the sense. Unless one has a keen desire for satsang, one cannot realise one's true identity.

Chapter 10, verse 145

Because of satsang bodily attachment is destroyed. It is satsang that breaks the cycle of births and deaths. It is satsang that gains the treasure of supreme energy and separates one from the worldly ties immediately.

Chapter 10, verse 148

To attain the highest state, the company of saints is purifying. If we surrender completely, our permanent peace is assured.

Chapter 10, verse 149

The saints manifest themselves to grant deliverance to people, who do not recite the name or bow down or have faith in them or sing their praises.

Chapter 10, verse 150

Ganga, Bhagirathi, Godavari, Krishna, Venya, Kaveri, Narmada – these rivers also desire that saints come and bathe in their waters so that they may touch their feet.

Chapter 10, verse 151

They wash the sins of the world (people). But they themselves are not freed from sins until they have touched the feet of saints.

Chapter 10, verse 152

In Satcharita, Hemadpant describes many incidents in which devotees get instant relief of their mental turmoil and attain peace and bliss by the mere darshan of Baba. Even a ferocious and sick tiger became calm and attained liberation by Baba's darshan.

Kakaji Vaidya of Vani

In Nasik district of Maharashtra there is a village called Vani. A famous temple of the Goddess Saptasringi is situated there. Kakaji Vaidya was the priest of that temple. He was in a disturbed state of mind due to insurmountable difficulties and was harassed by the worldly life. So he ardently prayed to the Goddess. The same night the Goddess appeared in his dream and advised him to go to Baba.

Thinking that Lord Tryambakeshwar was the Baba to whom the Goddess had referred, Kakaji went to the temple and worshipped the Lord for ten days. Every day he did the ritual abhisheka and pooja to the linga. But his mental troubles did not leave him. He returned to the Goddess's temple and asked the Goddess why she had sent him to Tryambakeshwar in vain and implored her to give him peace of mind.

That night the Goddess appeared in his dream again and clarified that she was talking about Shirdi's Sai Baba. Kakaji did not know where Shirdi was and who Sai Baba was. But before he could ask the Goddess, she disappeared. While Kakaji was worried about how he would go for Sai's darshan, Madhavarao Deshpande alias Shama came to the temple for fulfilling some vows. Later, both of them went to Shirdi. The priest bowed at Baba's feet and washed them with his tears. Hemadpant describes Kakaji's state:

Kakaji was filled with joy. After the darshan, his mind was at peace. He really became free of all worries, as the Cloud of Mercy had rained.

Chapter 30, verse 85

The fickleness of his mind disappeared. He was himself surprised. He wondered how strange this was!

Chapter 30, verse 86

Baba had not said a word. Nor had he asked any questions leading to this satisfaction. Nor had he given any blessings. The mere darshan had brought about contentment.

Chapter 30, verse 87

My fickle-mindedness has subsided by a mere darshan. I have attained incredible happiness and perfect understanding. This is called the greatness of satsang.

Chapter 30, verse 88

Somadeva Swamiji of Haridwar

Once the ascetic Somadeva swamiji came to Shirdi for Baba's darshan. Kaka Dixit's brother Bhaiji of Nagpur was his acquaintance and had arranged the trip. When the group reached Shirdi, they saw flags fluttering over the top of the masjid. All the other people who were with Somadeva swamiji lovingly bowed to the flags. But Somadeva swamiji's negative mind conjured sceptical ideas about Baba and he wanted to go back. He accused Baba of being hungry for fame and showing off pomp. Others told him to take Baba's darshan as they had almost reached Shirdi and there was no point turning back. They told him that Baba needed no flags nor popularity nor special honour. The flags were the symbols of the villagers' love for Baba.

Somadeva swamiji agreed to carry on. When he reached the masjid and saw Baba, his heart melted, his eyes filled with tears of love and his throat was choked. He experienced supreme bliss. His eyes were full of zest and joy and he felt anxious to roll in the dust of Baba's feet. The evil thoughts which had occurred earlier evaporated from his mind. The mind was enraptured with the joy of the darshan. He felt at peace and desired to stay there for ever. Supreme consciousness enveloped him. He was satisfaction personified. He recalled his own guru's words, 'Where the mind is fully absorbed that is our abode.' By Baba's grace he was purified and remained a staunch devotee of Baba till the end.

From these two incidents it is evident that whether supplicant or sceptic, both will get only one type of effect from the darshan of a saint – peace, satisfaction and bliss. Kakaji was dejected and Somadeva swamiji was cynical. Both were overpowered by the brilliance of the aura and glances of the saint. Kakaji got mental peace and steadiness of mind. Somadeva swamiji became free of vices and became able to recognise his real resting place. Other than these two states, cruelty and fierceness also get defeated by the blessings of the guru as shown in the description of the liberation of a tiger in chapter 31 Satcharita.

Liberation of a Sick Tiger

Once three men (dervishes) brought a sick tiger to Shirdi. They earned their livelihood by exhibiting the tiger from village to village. The tiger had fallen ill and they were not able to cure it. So they brought the tiger to Shirdi for Baba's darshan. The tiger was, naturally, fierce and frightful. It was in chains. When the tiger came in front of Baba, seeing his divine effulgence, it was taken aback and hung its head down with great reverence. As the tiger climbed the steps of the masjid, it looked at Baba with love. It fluffed the tuft of its tail and thrashed the ground thrice with it. It gave just one mighty roar and then fell dead at Sai's feet. Hemadpant says:

> Death in the presence of saints and sages is immensely meritorious, whether it be a worm, an insect or a tiger. All their sins are pardoned.
>
> Chapter 31, verse 143

> Anyone who dies while placing the head at the feet of a saint gets himself delivered and gains the benefits of a lifetime.
>
> Chapter 31, verse 145

> Unless one is very fortunate, can one merely leave the body in the presence of a saint? He will attain salvation.
>
> Chapter 31, verse 146

> It is immense bliss to leave one's body in the presence of a saint. Even the poison becomes nectar. Death is a pleasure not a sorrow.
>
> Chapter 31, verse 147

> One who dies in the presence of and at the feet of a saint is blessed and is merged into God, never to be born again.
>
> Chapter 31, verse 148

> Dying in the presence of saints is not death, but the bliss of heaven. He has won the transient world and has no worry about rebirth.
>
> Chapter 31, verse 149

One who leaves the body in the presence of saints does not return to this world. All the sins are pardoned by that, and he is rescued.

Chapter 31, verse 150

One who dies looking at a saint from the head to his toe nails, can that be called death? It is true self-realisation.

Chapter 31, verse 151

Even death is a blissful experience, if it is in front a saint. In that case, what more can be said about the greatness of satsang? As Hemadpant says:

The deeds of saints are impossible to comprehend. Their glories are beyond description. Who is capable of fully putting them in words?

Chapter 14, verse 31

Conclusion

All the scriptures and even gods extol the greatness of satsang. For human beings it is the only certain way to get jnanam. It leads them to the altar of self-realisation. Lord Krishna said that saints are his own essence and advises to resort to their feet. In *Yoga Vasishta*, Sage Vasishta repeatedly emphasises the greatness and essentiality of satsang. Sage Vasishta's companionship and preaching helped Lord Rama to rise above dualities of human existence and to overcome even the worst types of sorrows. Sage Medha's company and instructions helped King Suratha and the merchant Samadhi to overcome the setbacks in their personal lives. Obeying the sage's advice, they prayed ardently to the Goddess and fulfilled their wishes. So everyone should strive to keep good company – satsang.

Company of Saints

Bad company makes us a slave to passions and results in a sinful life. Satsang causes passions to disappear. Even in deep sleep, knowledge pulsates. Because of the saint's blessings, the twin fruits of self-denial and self-control are obtained. Saints open up the inner eyes of intellect and reveal the grandeur of the inner self. If we are able to get close to a saint, serve him and love him. If physical presence is not available, we can study the biographies and teachings of saints. By deep learning and meditation, we will get the same effect as of physical proximity.

The prerequisites for satsang are devotion, faith and patience. If we are fortunate to get satsang, we should guard and protect it throughout our life as a precious treasure. Just as an ant does not give up jaggery even if its neck is broken, we should stay with the saint's feet. Wholehearted surrender, obedience, service and patience will definitely give the desired results. Like the wish-fulfilling tree, the saint fulfils all the wishes of the devotees and wards off all miseries.

PURITY

He who tries to penetrate the realm of divine life without the purification of his mind, his efforts appear like an exhibition of scholarship. It is all futile effort.

> Chapter 17, verse 76

Unless the duties as fixed by the shastras are performed, the mind cannot be purified. Till the mind is not purified, know that true knowledge is not possible.

> Chapter 17, verse 44

By performance of one's duties, the mind will be purified. The concept of the oneness of the atman will be clear and this knowledge will protect like a shield against the dualities of passion and miseries of the material world.

> Chapter 20, verse 115

The intellect which regards everything as separate is actually due to ignorance. It needs to be purified by trisudhi. However, the advent of the guru purifies the mind and makes us realise our real self.

> Chapter 14, verse 41

16

PURITY

'Only from pure seedling, juicy and sweet fruits can come. Purity bears juicy and sweet fruits,' said Tukaram. This famous couplet has been tested by the people of Shirdi.

Chapter 10, verse 118

The literal meaning of purity is lack of contamination or taints. It mainly applies to physical objects and elements. For instance, impure water, impure air, impure gold, etc., mean that these items are polluted and not utilisable, or they are harmful if used. Any object which is inherently pure become impure by association with an impure entity. The state of purity and impurity is assessed based on the usefulness or harmfulness of a particular object. A pure object may be useful for good purposes. It creates pleasant and good effects or it may exist as featureless, and without any discernible qualities, but it never creates unrest or undesirable effects.

Purity originates from the quality of sattva and it does not have the property of mobility or tendency to create mobility. But impurity has the quality of rajas and hence it has mobility and it induces this in any object which comes in contact with it. So an impure object can overpower a pure object and mask its effects. For example, if a few drops of poison are dropped in a big glass of milk, the entire milk becomes poisonous. The milk is full glass and the poison is only a few drops, but still the effect of only the poison will be manifested. Air is all-pervading, but if a poisonous gas mixes with it, the entire air becomes harmful for breathing and if breathed, it may kill many within seconds. From this it is evident that any pure object, if it needs to be manifested in its own splendour, should exist in its own status or mix with like objects.

In mundane life, purity has the meaning of morality and ethics. A pure woman or man means she or he performs right actions in all aspects – in deeds, speech and in thoughts. In today's society anywhere in the world, in Kaliyuga, it is doubtful if we can find any pure human beings. All holy texts and teachings of all religions mention purity as the necessary quality to be upheld by all householders, as the family is the building blocks of a society. Human beings become impure by association with bad company.

In spirituality, purity means a mind which is devoid of vices like lust, anger, infatuation, greed, pride and jealousy, and an intellect which is not dictated by the ego. Such a being is full of the quality of sattva and is engaged in devotional practices. Purity is essential in obtaining the grace of God and guru.

Greatness of Purity

Hemadpant, while describing the meaning of dakshina (chapter 14) says that Prajapathi had three children – Devas (demigods), human beings and asuras (demons). He says that all three are human beings, but they differ in nature. Their character earns them their title. Devas imbibe their best virtues within themselves and exercise restraint. This means that they are endowed with excellent qualities and subdued senses. The demons resort to violence; they are wicked and harsh. Human beings are somewhere in the middle and are extremely avaricious. Devas attained their status mainly by self-control. So if a human being can control all impulses and behave virtuously, he will be a Deva. Purity gives tremendous inner strength. God and great souls bestow grace upon such a person, unasked. Such a pure person's thoughts manifest instantly, because the thoughts are always pure, selfless and based on full conviction. Their words become true because they originate from a pure, selfless mind. Lord Brahma is considered to be the creator of this visible world with all its constituents, including living and non-living things. This world exists perpetually because of his pure intention, which made him capable of doing such a great work. *Shri Gurucharitra* extols mother Anasuya as the epitome of purity. Because of her untainted service to her husband and mental purity, even nature and gods became subservient to her. Because of her inner purity, the Trinity Gods manifested as her son. That son is Jagad Guru Shri Lord Dattatreya. Purity is the foremost quality to be nurtured by anyone who aspires for spiritual progress.

How to Achieve Purity

Baba always insisted on purity in all aspect – body, mind and thoughts. For spiritual practices a strong body and mind is essential. Cleanliness keeps the body pure. Bathing three times a day was practised in old days. Keeping the body clean drives away diseases. Eating clean, nutritious food keeps the body healthy. Baba considered food as Brahman. He did not advocate fasting, but advised moderation in food. Excessive indulgence in food and enjoyments makes the body weak and diseased. He advised not to pamper the tongue and genitals. Moderation in sleep is essential for keeping the body healthy. A strong and healthy body, which is devoid of hankerings, can have a healthy mind which, in turn, harbours pure, sublime thoughts. We should also keep our surroundings clean and tidy so that our body does not contract any diseases from the environment.

Mental purity is essential for spiritual progress. It is the foremost requirement for realising the real knowledge or Brahman. How can mental purity be achieved? Hemadpant describes some ways to keep one's mind pure:

1. This ordinary material world of beings, movable and immovable objects, should not be taken into account at all. You should have full faith in God, who is the Supreme One.

Chapter 20, verse 119

Unflinching faith in God and living in God consciousness will purify the inner mind of a human being. Practising devotion by navavidha bhakti has a highly purifying effect. The ordinary material world has nothing to offer except confusion, impurity and delusions.

2. If you cannot comprehend this concept about this world and its nature, then at least try and give up the passion for accumulation of wealth, gold, etc.

Chapter 20, verse 120

If one cannot grasp the unreal nature of the visible world and the permanency of the Paramatman, he should at least not hanker for amassing wealth, gold and other physical assets. He should avoid greed, otherwise he will be preoccupied by the thoughts of money, will commit many wrong actions and suffer due to their consequences. This will lead to further downfall.

3. Even if this is impossible to practise then remember that you only have a right to action. Perform duties as long as you live, even if it be for a hundred years.

Chapter 20, verse 121

That should be practiced always in accordance with the doctrines prescribed by the scriptures, for example, agnihotra, etc., in the proper fashion, as per the caste and creed to which a person belongs, till the intellect becomes pure.

Chapter 20, verse 122

If one cannot follow the first two conditions, he can do his duties with a detached attitude so that he does not get bound to the effects of his actions. He can thus continue to perform his duties till the end of his life. But it should be in conformity with his occupation, position in the family, community and society. If he does not transgress any norms, his intellect will be unburdened.

4. This is one way of purification. The other is renunciation. But without practising either, only mundane knowledge will be collected and one will have to undergo all suffering as destined, which will chain you forever to the cycle of life and death.

Chapter 20, verse 123

The other way of achieving inner purification is renunciation of material life. Renunciation should be mental, not physical. Only a knowledgeable person who has the twin fruits of discrimination and detachment obtained from the tree of self-enquiry can renounce the physical world. If one does not practise proper mental renunciation, he will continue to suffer and this will lead to an unending cycle of births and deaths.

5. Even the mere darshan of saints is able to wash off all sins. How can the good fortune of those be described who are permanently in their company?

Chapter 20, verse 36

Impurity occurs mainly by association with impure elements. One should try to get pure inputs through all the senses. The company of saints is the most purifying association one can ever achieve, but it is very rare. It is only possible with God's grace and as a result of one's accumulated merits over many lifetimes. This emphasises the necessity for performing virtuous deeds.

6. Then you should see his miracle. The ocean of mercy, in the form of the guru, will be moved and will take you in his bed, swaying you lightly on the waves of kindness.

Chapter 17, verse 143

He will keep his hand of re-assurance on your head; will ward off bad omens; burn up heaps of all sins and anoint the forehead with Udi.

Chapter 17, verse 144

Obtaining the guru's grace is the greatest means of attaining mental purity. It can be obtained by sincere and selfless service and unconditional surrender. Even if a person had committed many sins, if he sincerely repent and take refuge at the feet of the guru with a sincere mind, the guru will bear his burden and make him free of all his sins. But if only outward gestures are there and the mind is still plagued by negativities and delusions, the guru's grace will be unattainable.

Hemadpant described some incidents which highlight the fact that Baba gave foremost importance to mental purity and he responded well to such pure souls.

Dr Pandit and Tripundra

Dr Pandit was Tatya Noolkar's friend. Once, he came to Shirdi and had Baba's darshan. Baba instructed him to go to Dada Kelkar's home. Later, when Dada Kelkar went to the masjid for aarati, he took Dr Pandit with him. Dr Pandit bowed down at Baba's feet. He took the plate containing sandalwood paste from Dada's hands and lovingly drew a tripundra on Baba's forehead. Baba did not object. Dada Kelkar was surprised as Baba had never allowed anybody to apply sandalwood paste on his forehead. Only Mhalasapathy used to apply it on his throat and others applied it to his feet. Dada felt offended and he questioned Baba about such partisan act. Baba told him that Dr Pandit considered Baba as his own guru and did the worship. He never had any discriminative thoughts in his mind and Baba was won over by his pure intent.

Cholkar and Sugarless Tea

Cholkar was a poor man who had many household responsibilities. He did not have a permanent job. Once he happened to listen to Das Ganu's kirtan. He mentally prayed to Baba that if his job became permanent, he would go to Shirdi and distribute sugar candy in Baba's name. Soon, his job was made permanent. But because of his expense burdens, he could not save money for the journey. Wanting to fulfil his promise as soon as possible, he gave up sugar in his diet to save money. He started to drink tea without sugar. After sometime he managed to save money and go to Shirdi. He bowed down at the feet of Baba and offered sugar candy. He sat humbly in front of Baba. When he got up to leave along with his host, Jog, Baba told Jog to give Cholkar tea with plenty of sugar. This showed that he knew about Cholkar's secret penance which was now over.

Hemadpant says that covetous people make big promises of donating gold and feeding many Brahmins for achieving their selfish interests. Cholkar was poor, but he felt the inner agony when he was unable to fulfil his promise quickly. Knowing his inner state, Baba blessed him by giving him his love.

Purity springs from mental actions, not necessarily from performing physical acts. The attitude and intention behind the act determine the purity of the act. Reactions to actions depend upon the imagination and understanding. If both are pure and harmonious, no argument or fight happens. Hemadpant describes such an incident in chapter 24.

Mavshibai and Anna Chinchanikar

Mavshibai was an aged widow. One day she was serving Baba in the masjid by massaging Baba's abdomen and sides. She was vigorous in her service and hence she was moving up and down. Anna Chinchanikar, a simple, straightforward devotee, was standing outside the railing and pressing Baba's left hand gently and he was steady. Mavshibai, in the bliss of her service to Baba, was swaying and her face came near Anna's. Witty Mavshibai asked Anna whether he was asking for a kiss and whether he had no consideration for his old age. Anna became angry and shouted at Mavshibai saying that it was she who brought her face near his. Then Baba intervened and asked Anna, 'Why are you unnecessarily raising this hue-and-cry? I do not understand what impropriety is there when the mother is kissed.' Just as there is love between mother and son, if that same loving feeling had existed between both of them, then this situation would not have arisen and there would be no question of feeling of anger.

Effect of Company

Mental purity is the foremost requisite for spiritual progress and self-realisation. Association with the wrong kind of persons is the primary contributing factor for impurity. In this context I am reminded of a fable.

In a forest there was a parrot couple. Two chicks hatched in their nest. One day, a hunter caught those chicks and sold one of them to an ascetic and the other one to a butcher. Both the brother-chicks grew up in homes of their respective masters. The ascetic named his chick as Rama and the butcher named his chick as Durmukha. When they grew up, they flew away from their cages. Rama parrot made a nest on a mango tree and Durmukha made his nest on a nearby banyan tree. One day a wayfarer came that way. He was tired in hot sun. He came near the banyan tree and thought of resting under its shade. Durmukha parrot saw him and started calling other birds. 'Oh, birds, one human being has come near our tree. We should pierce his eyes with our beaks and wound his neck and cut it.' The traveller heard these words and fled in fear. He went near the mango tree. Rama parrot saw him and called other birds and said, 'Look, a human being has come near the tree. He is tired. Let us spread tender leaves so that he can rest on them and let us drop ripe mangoes for him to eat.' The surprised wayfarer asked the parrot how both the parrots could behave in exactly opposite manner. Rama parrot replied, 'We are brothers. I grew up in an ascetic's ashrama and saw how he treated his guests with kindness and courtesy. I grew up hearing the kind and sweet words uttered by the ascetic and his disciples. My brother grew up in the house of a butcher and grew up seeing his master's cruel acts – killing animals and severely punishing servants and disrespecting guests. He could only hear the harsh and rude words uttered by the fighter and his household inmates. That is why we behave in different manner.'

The fable is quoted here to highlight the fact that living environments and interactions are the major contributing factors for mental purity. Members of each family and society should strive to nurture pure qualities in themselves and others.

Conclusion

Mental purity is the foremost prerequisite for spiritual progress because it enables us to receive the grace of guru and God. Holy company makes us pure in all aspects and enable us to search for the real purpose of life. Thus, mental purity should be achieved at any cost because it is essential for a life free of conflicts. It makes our life peaceful and congenial for advancement in spiritual practices.

The three inherent flaws of human mind are impurity, confusion and a veil of ignorance. The feeling of 'I' and 'mine' and the inability to see the unity of the universe is the predominant impurity. Desires, passions and delusions are other impurities. Company of bad people and interactions with them makes us impure. Selfless service to all fellow beings, company of saints and wise souls, sincere service and unconditional surrender to our guru removes mental impurities. Confusion is the tossing of mind among objects of love and hatred. The mind becomes a prey to fear through its fluctuations. The confusion of mind is removed by worship of God and guru and following yogic practices. The veil of ignorance is removed when real knowledge dawns. Study of holy scriptures, meditation and continuous contemplation of pure consciousness help in achieving jnanam.

GURU'S GREATNESS

The name of the guru and the intimate association with the guru, the grace of the guru and the milk-like sacred water which has washed his feet; the sacred mantra from the guru and residence in his household – these could be obtained with great efforts only.

Chapter 1, verse 58

The association with the guru is like the sacred Ganges water which cleanses and makes one pure. It also stabilises the mind on God which otherwise is fickle.

Chapter 1, verse 60

Such is the marvel of guru's grace that it makes a dry and stiff plant effortlessly and profusely blossom in the most arid soil.

Chapter 3, verse 240

The devotees of the guru experience, on resorting to his feet with full faith, that not only guru, but Parabrahman is moved. Such is the marvel of guru pooja.

Chapter 11, verse 9

The path of the world is full of confusion and dim. The words of the guru shine like rays from a lamp to make it smooth and perceivable.

Chapter 18, verse 19

GURU'S GREATNESS

Honour the words of the guru and give him a seat in your heart with faith. With complete resolution and abandoning all aspirations let us worship him with only this desire.

Chapter 11, verse 7

In mundane life we all are familiar with teacher–student concept. This relates to the teaching and learning of physical sciences and skills which help people obtain livelihood. But in spirituality, the teacher is known as guru who teaches the real knowledge. Guru is the one who preaches about the knowledge of the Parabrahman, removes the darkness of the lack of this knowledge and helps in unifying our soul with the Parabrahman. The Sanskrit word 'guru' itself represents who is guru and what he does.

The letter *G* represents grantor of all success.

The letter *G* also represents Lord Ganapathi, who is the remover of all obstacles.

The letter *U* represents the imperceptible Lord Vishnu.

The letter *R* represents Lord Agni (Fire) who is the vanquisher of all evils.

Guru's Greatness

The greatness of the guru is indescribable because guru is Parabrahman itself. Parabrahman cannot be described by words. Parabrahman can only be experienced by becoming one with it. Guru is the person who has realised the Parabrahman by direct experience and lives in it. Such a person helps others have the same experience. Realising Parabrahman and living the whole life in that state is possible only for great sadgurus – not possible even for the Trinity Gods. So even the Trinity Gods – Brahma, Vishnu, Maheswar – bow down at the feet of the sadguru. If gods become angry at a person, no one in the three worlds can save that person, except the guru. That is the greatness of the guru.

In *Dasabodha*, Saint Ramadas describes the origin of universe as follows:

The visible world is unreal and illusory. It arose as a temporary conceptualisation in Parabrahman. This notion gave rise to the visible world. Although the notion emanated from Parabrahman, it remained as it was without any changes whatsoever even during the fraction of time during which the concept came. The feeling which the Parabrahman had is known as the 'Original Maya', which has two integral parts. The first one is pure and completely knowledgeable and the other one signifies the ultimate power and has many facets. The first one represents God as we know and speak about. The second one is called 'Maya'. Maya manifests as the universe and makes everything from its own basic elements by a process called pancheekaranam. The common person experiences only the universe and happenings in it which are the creations of Maya and hence are nothing but illusions. But saints and sages always experience the Parabrahman.

The sadguru functions as a boat for his disciples to cross the ocean of Maya and reach the other shore – Parabrahman. Who can extol enough the greatness of such a sadguru?

Hemadpant says:

> The sadguru dwells far beyond what is known as the 'Maya', which that Brahmand creates here and which is invisible or illusory.
>
> Chapter 1, verse 47
>
> The Vedas have been unable to describe his greatness and are therefore silent. The devices and niceties of evidence fail.
>
> Chapter 1, verse 48
>
> The Vedas and Shrutis remain silent in their efforts to praise you. Whence can I have the intelligence to try and praise you or understand you?
>
> Chapter 1, verse 52
>
> Brahma's brahmand cannot exist without the sadguru. I offer my five pranas to you and with total dedication surrender to you for protection.
>
> Chapter 1, verse 54
>
> The guru is the real mother and father. Since numerous births, he is the guardian and protector. He is Brahma–Vishnu–Sankar, the doer and the one who gets everything done.
>
> Chapter 25, verse 60

So to write or describe the greatness of guru is humanly impossible. Even Lord Maheswar praises the sadguru in *Guru Gita*. Lord Maheswar says:

> Whatever stage of life to which one belongs, whatever caste or creed or country to which one belongs, renouncing fame, name and property, one should serve the guru with oneness, finding in him the unity.

Lord Krishna also extols the greatness of the guru. The Lord says:

Remembrance of the sadguru is the surest way to please me, who is Narayana. Singing the praises of the sadguru rather than my praises is dearer to me a thousand-fold. Such is the excellence of and the profound significance of the sadguru.

Hence to describe the greatness of the guru is an impossible task. Even to compile what Hemadpant had described in Satcharita is also a mammoth task. Only with the guru's grace can we sing or write about his glories. Whatever I could assimilate and present in this writing is being done by Shri Shirdi Sai Baba himself. I am just an instrument. So, whatever merits or faults, all belong to Baba.

Types of Gurus

Hemadpant describes two types of gurus – niyata guru and aniyata guru. Then he describes the greatness of sadguru. Lastly, he warns the devotees that the world is full of false gurus and a seeker should be able to recognise them and shun them altogether.

Aniyata Guru: Aniyata guru is an occasional teacher. He stresses the development of the divine qualities and purification of the mind. He can also show the path to moksha. So aniyata guru can only instruct about God.

Niyata Guru: Niyata guru is decided by destiny. Niyata guru is a permanent teacher. He understands the nature and needs of his pupils and moulds them in such a way that the two-fold nature of self disappears and they become one with God. He gives witness to the great statement that 'God and yourself are not different.'

Sadguru: The guru who brings his students to realise their own nature is known as the sadguru. In chapter 48,

Hemadpant narrates the characteristics of the sadguru as follows:

> He who has full knowledge of the shastras, is fully experienced and can give practical knowledge, alone is qualified to instruct the disciple. Such a person is called a sadguru.
>
> Chapter 48, verse 8
>
> Know that he is the sadguru who does not, even in his dream, expect any service or profit from his disciple. On the contrary, he wishes to serve the disciple.
>
> Chapter 48, verse 10
>
> Only such a sadguru is beneficial who does not consider that a disciple is insignificant and the guru is the best among all. He should be egoless.
>
> Chapter 48, verse 11
>
> He believes that the disciple is Purnabrahman and treats him as his own son. He does not expect anything from him for his maintenance. Such a sadguru is best in the world.
>
> Chapter 48, verse 12
>
> He who is the abode of supreme peace, has no pride of learning, does not distinguish between the young and the old, and the rich and the poor, is the embodiment of the sadguru.
>
> Chapter 48, verse 130

A disciple or a devotee should approach only a true guru because the world is full of false or hypocritical gurus. Hemadpant describes the characteristics of false gurus also:

Many such gurus are there who collect a number of disciples around them and who forcefully give a mantra in the ear (secretly), merely to make money.

Chapter 10, verse 61

They teach their disciples righteousness but their own behaviour is contrary. How will they help them to cross the worldly ocean and avoid life and death?

Chapter 10, verse 62

Today, many people pose as gurus and exploit innocent people. They create illusory objects and exhibit superhuman deeds. Such jugglery and hypnotism are not spirituality. Some may have great oratory skills to describe about nonduality, but they themselves are terribly attracted to organic pleasures. Such people should be avoided.

Such people have great pomp and show, but do not have real, tender love. They have no actual experience. We should not submit before those who do not teach the disciple how to control the senses and remain continuously in sadhana. Such gurus are useless.

Hemadpant describes what kind of relationship should exist between the guru and disciple or sishya.

The greatness of Guru–Sishya Relationship

The relationship between the guru and the disciple is that of a father and son. The guru is both father and mother for the disciple. The guru is the protector and friend. The guru is everything for the disciple. Hemadpant describes Baba's love for disciples and devotees as that of a mother bird and mother tortoise. In chapter 15 he says that the more the devotee clings to Mother Sai with love and affection, the more Sai loves him, disregarding all the discomforts. He explains this by citing the beautiful example of how a mother cat feeds her new-borns.

If a cat has just fed her new-borns and goes out, then when she returns, her kittens longingly return to her, and again and again rush to her with love to suckle.

Chapter 15, verse 12

Then she gets fed up and growls which quietens the babies for a while. No sooner than the mother cat is quietly resting, they circle around her and again suckle.

Chapter 15, verse 13

When they lovingly nudge and suck, milk flows out of the mother cat. Then she forgets her earlier growling and spreads herself on the ground with love.

Chapter 15, verse 14

As her love overpowers her reluctance, she clings to her own babies with her four legs tightly; again and again licks them and fondles them. Oh! what a wonderful sight it is!

Chapter 15, verse 15

As her abdomen is scratched by their sharp nails, her love increases and the milk flows more abundantly.

Chapter 15, verse 16

Just as those babies' love and affection makes the mother give more milk, your devotion at the feet of Sai will melt his heart.

Chapter 15, verse 17

The guru protects the disciple just as a mother bird protects her chicks and keeps them under her wings. Sometimes Sai acts just like a mother tortoise. Mother tortoise lays eggs on the seashore and returns back to the sea. But her mind and thoughts are with the eggs. The eggs hatch and the hatchlings do not get the physical presence of the mother. But they constantly remember their mother and the mother casts her glances from afar. Thus the hatchlings sustain by remembering the mother and the mother transmits nourishment through her glances.

Baba Describes about the Love of His Own Guru

Baba himself had described the love and affection of his own guru:

> I lived at his feet for 12 years. The guru brought me up from childhood. There was never a dearth of food and clothing and he nurtured immeasurable love for me.
>
> Chapter 19, verse 61

> He was the embodiment of love and devotion and had genuine affection for a disciple. A guru like mine would rarely be found. I cannot describe the rapturous joy.
>
> Chapter 19, verse 62

> How could I describe that love! When I look at him, he seemed as if he was in deep meditation and we both were filled with bliss. I could never look anywhere else.
>
> Chapter 19, verse 63

> I would go on looking affectionately at the face of the guru, day and night. I knew no hunger or thirst. My mind would get restless without the guru.
>
> Chapter 19, verse 64

He was the only object of my meditation. I would have no other goal than him. He alone was my constant goal. The ways of the guru are mysterious.

Chapter 19, verse 65

This was the only expectation of my guru. He did not desire anything more than this. He never disregarded me and always protected me from difficulties.

Chapter 19, verse 66

Sometimes I would stay close to his feet, and sometimes away from him. But I was never deprived of the closeness of his company. He looked after me with love and care.

Chapter 19, verse 67

From this description it is clear that the only thing guru expects from the disciple is total focus and meditation on the guru. The disciple's sole aim should be to constantly meditate on the guru. The guru in turn nurtures and nourishes the disciple with unparalleled love.

When the disciple is under the protective wings of the guru, even the toughest ordeals ordained by the guru will be very blissful. In chapter 32, Baba describes how he met his guru in a forest and how the guru took him near a well and suspended him over the well-water. After four or five hours the guru returned and took him out. He asked Baba whether he was fine. Baba replied:

I was in supreme bliss. The joy I experienced is beyond my poor powers to describe.

Chapter 32, verse 73

Guru's Greatness

How wonderful was the Guru's school! I became detached from my parent's love and the chains of greed and love stopped. I attained salvation easily.

Chapter 32, verse 76

Nothing appears impossible. My evil tendencies vanished. My previous karmas were wiped out. I thought I should embrace this Guru's neck and remain staring at him always.

Chapter 32, verse 77

If his image was not reflected in the eyes, then they were only balls of flesh! Better still, I would have preferred to be blind. Such was the effect of the guru's school on me.

Chapter 32, verse 78

Which unfortunate individual would have wanted to leave the precincts of this school having once entered it? My guru was my mother, my father, my property – everything to me.

Chapter 32, verse 79

By the grace of the guru, realisation flashed upon me by itself, without effort or study. I had not to seek anything but everything became clear to me as broad daylight.

Chapter 32, verse 89

Through these verses Baba explains the effect of guru's love and care. The disciple realises that all other relations and their love could never be equal to the love he experiences from the guru. He gets mentally freed from the shackles of the mundane relations. Since he does not foster no memories other than related to the guru, he gets freed from his previous karmas. Vicious qualities disappear from him. He longs only for the company of the guru and depends solely on the guru for his sustenance. He mentally renounces everything and lives only for being in the presence of the guru. Then the guru's grace works on his inner realms and the real knowledge flashes on him without any efforts.

Only a Sadguru can have such an effect on a devotee or disciple. So, devotees should be able to recognise a real guru and resort to him for their spiritual progress.

Guru's Grace

Sadguru is Parabrahman. All the worlds and all the gods are subservient to him. He can bestow everything to his devotees or disciples– material welfare, spiritual progress, self-realisation and liberation – depending on the depth of devotion and faith. The guru considers the disciple's eagerness, longing and sincerity to follow the teachings. For his devotees, the guru is the celestial cow Kamadhenu and the celestial tree Kalpavruksha. But the guru's main mission is to help his disciples to realise their true nature and become one with the Parabrahman. This is also the ultimate purpose of human life.

By the guru's grace the disciple achieves the state of oneness, where the meditator, meditation and the object being meditated all become one. The disciple becomes desireless and detached from mundane sensory pleasures. The guru works on the inner self of the disciple. He becomes the boat to transport the disciple to the shore of Parabrahman, sailing through the fierce waters of physical existence which are infested with whirlpools, sharks and crocodiles, that is, vices such as greed, enmity, pride, malice, avarice, contentiousness, attachment, passions and so on. The disciple achieves complete tranquillity, peace and bliss. The fierce, roaring material life, which is inside his mental realm, is completely pacified and the inner consciousness shines. He abides in a blissful state and realises that it is the state of Parabrahman. Thus no external calamities will affect him, because the guru has bestowed him the real knowledge.

A sadguru can make a disciple realise the self within moments or after a certain period. He can transfer his powers to his devotee or disciple instantaneously through a word, touch or looks – what is called 'shaktipath'.

Hemadpant says that the atman is bound in the body just like a parrot is foolishly enjoying inside a cage. But when the guru touches, the awakening by shaktipath causes the inner eyes to open and the parrot breaks open the web of desires and reclaims its freedom.

The realisation that the Parabrahman and soul are one is the ultimate goal of human life. Once the self-knowledge is achieved, nothing more remains to be understood. Self-knowledge enables us to understand the material world as well as we understand the palm of our hand. The fruit of realisation is renunciation of the world without hesitation. Immediate heavenly bliss is attained and the person achieves salvation. Only a sadguru can impart the knowledge of the atman and the supreme self.

> If anyone else except the guru imparts knowledge, it will not be able to liberate you from the world; neither will it at all be possible of leading to the fruits of moksha nor will it ever have the full impact on your mind.
> Chapter 17, verse 139

Therefore, knowledge is not possible to be obtained without a guru. All the learned men are aware of this that only the capable feet of the guru can solve the mystery of the Brahman and the atman.
Chapter 17, verse 140

Hemadpant says:

> Innumerable stars of one's own intellect and imagination will not enable one to escape the eighty-four lakh cycles of births and deaths. Only one moon, the teacher, well versed in the sacred knowledge, is enough. When he is there, there will not be trace of darkness.
>
> Chapter 16, verse 123

> That which is not acquired by many with a lot of efforts will be acquired easily if one clings fast to a sadguru who spreads the light of good teaching.
>
> Chapter 16, verse 124

Conclusion

Guru and Parabrahman are one and the same. The greatness of the guru cannot be described. The guru purifies the disciple, opens his inner vision and enables him to realise the Parabrahman. The guru's method of teaching and imparting knowledge is very personal. The disciple or devotee should get rid of ego and pride and completely surrender at the guru's feet. Then the guru will impart the divine knowledge and nothing more will remain for the disciple to know and understand. They can live in the world, yet not be a part of it and finally they will merge with the Pure Consciousness. Hence, the guru is the most venerable. The guru–sishya relationship is the only real relationship existing in this world and it is the most sacred one.

DISCIPLESHIP

He did not consider the propriety or impropriety of the Guru's orders, but carried them out meticulously. He did even the menial duties for the Guru such as carrying water.

Chapter 5, verse 127

Have firm faith in him who is your own guru; it should not be anywhere else. Bear in mind this deep meaning.

Chapter 12, verse 176

Though a guru is very powerful, he expects only wisdom from his disciple, firm faith, lots of courage and patience at the feet of the guru.

Chapter 19, verse 58

One who is always ready to serve the Guru, respect and obey the guru's orders, makes the guru responsible for what is correct or incorrect in all respects.

Chapter 23, verse 141

He is the servant of the guru's orders. He does not think independently. Always obeying the orders of the guru, he does not distinguish what is good or bad.

Chapter 23, verse 142

To completely obey the guru's orders, that is the meaning of discipleship for a disciple. That is our jewel. Disobedience is the greatest sin.

Chapter 23, verse 172

18

DISCIPLESHIP

As gold and its glitter, or lamp and its light, so is the state of complete unity between the guru and disciple.

Chapter 5, verse 134

The follower of a preceptor or guru is known as a disciple. The disciple follows the guru's instructions and serves him so that the guru will enable him to realise his real nature and Paramatman. In mundane life, there are teachers and students for imparting and learning physical sciences. All these branches of learning remain separate from the learners even when they become an expert in it. But in spirituality, the guru's instructions enable the disciples to seek the truth and once they realise it, they become one with it. In *Viveka Chudamani*, Shri Sankaracharya describes who is qualified to seek self-realisation and how they should proceed. Human life is the best form for seeking self-realisation. Being a Brahmin is an advantage, but by Brahmin it is meant not the caste but a person in whom the quality of purity (sattva) predominates. Such a person should cultivate discrimination, dispassion, discipline and desire for liberation. Then that person should seek and identify a real guru. A real guru is selfless and does not expect any favours from the disciple. A real guru preaches about the knowledge of the Paramatman, removes the darkness of the lack of this knowledge and helps in unifying the disciple's soul with the Paramatman. Such a guru teaches the disciple how to remain in sadhana and how to control the senses. If the guru's behaviour and teachings are not in conformity with these characteristics, the seeker should not accept him as guru.

After approaching a real guru, the disciple should obediently serve the guru. Then the guru will help him to realise the Paramatman which resides inside the disciple's own heart as pure consciousness but has forgotten its real nature and become inert. The guru's instructions help the disciple realise his own real nature by removing the impurity of ignorance, but the disciple should necessarily have the previously-mentioned qualities – discrimination, dispassion, discipline and desire for liberation. Once the disciple develops these qualities, he will have wisdom and will be ready to receive the guru's instructions. His intelligence will be awakened and his mind will be fully ready to be occupied by the guru and the sacred scriptures. He will get the spirit of enquiry into truth and desire for its realisation.

Guru and Disciple: The True Relationship

The relationship between the guru and the disciple is the most versatile and the only true and real relationship that exists in this world. All other relationships are illusory and unreal. Once a disciple surrenders to the guru, that relationship is eternal. The disciples can also absorb teachings which are conducive to their inner transformation from other preceptors and scriptures. But their original guru is their one and only master. This is the basic and important prerequisite for perfect discipleship.

In *Shri Gurucharitra*, there is a story of a gurudrohi Brahmin. He left his own guru and approached Shri Narasimhasaraswathi Swami. He left his guru because of the hardships to which he was subjected. He was not keen on obeying his guru's orders. Shri Narasimhasaraswathi

Swami advised him about the importance of following the guru's words and commands by giving an example of a story from Adiparva of Mahabharata. He convinced him about the consequences of the heinous action of deserting his guru and sent him back. There are many incidents in Satcharita where Baba insists on the fact that a disciple should never leave his own guru.

The Devotee Pant's Experience

Once a devotee named Pant went to Shirdi on the request of his child's father-in-law and mother-in-law and some friends whom he had met on a train. He was already graced by his guru and attached to him. At first, he was hesitant to go to Shirdi. But he did not like to displease his relatives and friends. So he took permission from his guru and came to Shirdi. When he had Baba's darshan, he had a fit and he fell down unconscious. With Baba's grace and help from other devotees, he regained full consciousness after some water was sprinkled on his forehead. Baba, being omniscient, knew that he was a disciple of another guru, assured him and confirmed his faith in his own guru. Baba said, 'Come what may, leave not your bolster (support, which is the guru). Remain steady always, always be one with him.'

A disciple should never waver in his devotion to his guru. There may be many other gurus. They may be appear to be better than his own guru. But he should not leave his guru and go after other gurus. He should not compare others' achievement with his own and get troubled in the heart. Even though his guru may not be in a physical body, once he has surrendered, it is for the whole lifetime and also for life after life. The disciple only needs to have faith and devotion at his guru's feet and meditate on him. Baba once said, 'There are innumerable saints in the world, but our father is the real Father (real guru).'

Anandrao Pakhade's Dream

Kaka Dikshit used to do parayana of religious scriptures during and also after Baba's samadhi. One day he was doing the parayana of *Bhagavatam* at Kaka Mahajani's house. Some devotees, including Shama, were listening to it. Kaka Dikshit read about the story related to the nine pious ascetics of Rishabha lineage, that is, the Nine Naths. Kaka Dikshit was greatly influenced by the devotion of the Nine Naths. Kaka Dikshit became restless thinking that he would never be able to achieve the kind of devotion that the Nine Naths had practised. Shama tried to pacify him saying that it was futile for a person, who had the good fortune of having a jewel like Baba, to worry like that. He also said that chanting the name of God and guru was the means for overcoming the fear of mundane existence.

But Kaka Dikshit could not be pacified. He was continuously thinking about the devotion of the Nine Naths. The next day, while he was doing the parayana, Anandrao Pakhade came and sat near Shama and told him about a dream-vision he had the previous night. Kaka Dikshit asked them what they were discussing. Anandrao narrated his dream:

I was standing in an ocean in waist-deep water. Shri Samartha appeared before me, all of a sudden. Madhavarao was also standing there and told me to bow down at Baba's feet. I told him that since the feet are under the water, I could not do so. Then Shama requested Baba to draw his feet out of the water. Baba drew out his feet and without delay I bowed to them. Baba blessed me and assured my welfare. He also told me to give a silk-bordered dhoti to Shama and said that I would be profited by that.

Hence Anandrao had brought a silk-bordered dhoti to give to Shama. Since Shama wanted to get further confirmation before accepting the dhoti, they drew lots. It was confirmed that Shama should accept it. Thus, Kaka's doubts were cleared. Hemadpant says:

One should think for oneself about the essence of this whole story. Once there is a surrender to the guru, then one must follow the guru's instructions.

Chapter 45, verse 111

The guru knows better than us, from head to toe, our stage of development, our part in life and our inclinations. He is the means of the final salvation.

Chapter 45, verse 112

The diagnosis depends on the disease and accordingly the medications and antidotes are given. The sadguru always lays down what is suitable for the disciple's sickness of existence to be cured.

Chapter 45, verse 113

Do not imitate the guru and the way in which the guru conducts himself. Only revere and obey the instructions that he gives you.

Chapter 45, verse 114

Concentrate on his words. Meditate upon them regularly. Bear it in mind that those words will be the cause of your upliftment.

Chapter 45, verse 115

Listen to whatever anyone else says. But do not let it divert your attention. Do not forget your own guru's words.

Chapter 45, verse 122

In short, love your guru. Whole-heartedly surrender to him. Just as there is no darkness before the sun, there is no sea of mundane existence for you to cross.

Chapter 45, verse 124

> Wherever you are in the world, near or however far, even beyond the seven seas, the guru is extremely loving towards the devotee.
>
> Chapter 45, verse 125

Firm Faith and Patience at the Feet of the Guru

Once an old lady was keen on acquiring a mantra from Sai and began fasting. She said she will continue her fast until Baba gave her a mantra. Shama informed Baba about the condition of the woman and requested him to say something to her to convince her to give up her fast. Baba called her and told her that he also had a guru, but he did not receive any mantra from his guru. The guru asked only two pice from him – faith (shraddha) and patience (saburi). The disciple should have complete faith and remain at the feet of the guru. He should remain in the meditation of his guru. The guru should be his constant goal. Baba told her:

> You should regard me as the whole and sole. I will also regard you in the same way. My guru did not teach me anything else at all.
>
> Chapter 19, verse 73

The disciples should never aim to receive fulfilment of any desires from guru. They should have unwavering faith in the guru, constantly meditate on the guru and stay patiently at the feet of the guru without any anxieties or ambitions. Then the guru will also think of them as his own and protect them by every means. Once the disciple is mature enough to receive the fruits of the grace of the guru, the guru will transmit it. Until their faults and defects get corrected and the disciples become pure and mature, the guru will not impart full grace. Until the right time arrives, the disciple should serve the guru with patience, obey and fulfil each and every order of the guru and wait courageously.

Obedience to the Guru

Obedience is the best ornament of a disciple and the means to receive the guru's grace.

The disciples should serve their guru whole-heartedly. In this regard Hemadpant describes three kinds of disciples – the best, the middling and the base. The best disciple anticipates the guru's desire and on realising it, begins to carry it out without waiting for a specific order. The middling disciple obeys the guru's order, to its letter, without any delay. The base disciple procrastinates carrying out the guru's command, even though given repeatedly and commits mistakes at every step. To highlight the fact that a disciple should implicitly obey the guru's order even if it seems to be totally unacceptable or laborious or contrary to common belief systems, Baba once tested Kaka Dikshit and showed to others that he was an ideal disciple.

Once somebody brought a goat which looked feeble and on the point of death. Baba asked Bade Baba to kill the goat. Bade Baba asked why the goat should be killed unnecessarily. Baba asked Madhavarao to bring a knife. With a troubled heart he brought a knife from Radhakrishnabai. But when Radhakrishnabai came to know about the matter, she took the knife back because she felt pity on the goat. Madhavarao went to find another knife but remained in the wada, delaying his return so that he would not have to kill the goat. So Baba sent Kaka Dikshit to bring a knife. He brought the knife. Baba ordered him to kill the goat in one stroke. When he was about to kill the goat, Baba said, 'Oh, Kaka, stop this. How cruel you are! Have you no thought about this?' Kaka threw away the knife and said that obeying the guru's order is the only creed of the followers. It is their Veda and shastra. He continued:

Virtue or sin of killing or non-killing are meaningless to us. Our salvation is at the sadguru's feet. Why should we think of the reason behind the order?

Chapter 23, verse 175

Disobeying the order of the guru is to cause degradation of life; obeying the order of the guru is the main plank of righteousness.

Chapter 23, verse 177

We do not know fame or calamity. We do not know selfishness or the welfare of others. We only know to perform the work stated by the guru. That is the goal of our life.

Chapter 23, verse 179

Compared to the guru's command, the precepts and prohibitions are like a fool's prattling. If one's only aim and duty is to follow the guru's command, the disciples' problems are the concern of the guru.

Chapter 23, verse 180

Through this leela Baba wanted to make everyone realise that total obedience to the guru is the foremost quality a disciple should have in order to progress forward. Even Lord Krishna and Lord Rama also served their respective gurus very humbly. Baba himself used to talk about his own guru very reverentially and how he meditated on his guru and how he forgot all other relations, being in the guru's school. He served Jawahar Ali when the latter told him to be his disciple. Even though Baba was Paramatman incarnate and he knew very well about Jawahar's defects, he served him obediently and did even menial works for him.

Conclusion

A disciple should nurture devotion to God and the guru. He should always be in union with his own guru. He should nurture firm faith and patience at the feet of his guru. He should be humble, obedient and courageous. He should respect other preceptors and spiritual cultures. The disciples should avoid useless arguments and talks. He should neither engage in debate nor try to establish his views or refute others' opinions. Instead, he should concentrate on his own well-being. He should avoid base feelings like enmity, malice, anger, lust, pride, jealousy and so on. He should uphold moral values and control his mind, senses and speech. He should always remember his guru.

He should realise that the guru is the embodiment of all gods. But this realisation will occur only as a result of the guru's grace. Baba encouraged spiritual ways and rituals of the particular sect to which a particular devotee belonged. It helped the disciple not to get distracted from the goal and nurtured inner purity and peace. So a disciple should continue to practise navavidha bhakti and study the scriptures. But in his heart, he should be convinced that the guru is Paramatman and all his spiritual practices and devotion would reach the feet of the guru and that it is the guru who is helping him in his sadhana. Such a realisation will occur in the disciples when they patiently serve the guru selflessly and when all their defects have come to naught. Baba himself encouraged his devotees and disciples to read and meditate on many spiritual scriptures – be it Hindu scriptures or scriptures of other religions. He gave darshan to many devotees as their favourite gods and as other gurus. It strengthened their devotion and faith.

In this present age, the ancient custom of guru-sishya relationship is not possible in the physical sense, because the time is not conducive for functioning of gurukul. The social systems, human behaviour and the needs of life have

Discipleship

changed. Genuine gurus and disciples are scarce. But if there are genuine spiritual aspirants, definitely they will get the inner guidance from Baba. He will provide all the necessary circumstances. If an aspirant lives according to the requisites, Baba will definitely help him or her achieve the goal of human life, that is, self-realisation. They do not need to give up the world and live in the jungles or Himalayas. They can continue to stay in their family and in the society. They should make their own inner environment an ashrama or gurukul and their heart the seat of Baba. They should offer their mind and thoughts at the feet of Baba and live their life as Baba directed the person who had asked for the knowledge of Brahman. Then they should wait patiently. At right time, Baba's grace will descend on them. What such a person achieves will be far more superior than living in the Himalayas or any physical ashrama.

BIBLIOGRAPHY

Bhagavatapuranam, English translation by Bhaktivedanta Swami Prabhupada, 2014.

Dasabodha by Saint Samartha Ramadas, English translation by Baba Belsare, 2010.

Devi Mahatmyam, Hindi translation, Gita Press, Gorakhpur, 2010.

Guru Charitra, English, Shri Swami Samarth Viswa Kalyan Kendra, 2008.

Lord Shri Dattatreya, The Trinity, Dwarika Mohan Mishra, 2012.

Shri Dnyaneswari, English translation of the Marathi original by Diwakar Ghaisas, First edition.

Shri Gurusamhita, English translation of the Sanskrit original by Dr Narasimha Banavare, First edition.

Shri Sai Samartha Satcharita, English translation of the Marathi original by Zarine, Fourth edition.

Tripurarahasyam, English translation by Swami Shri Ramananda Saraswathi, 2002.

Vasishta's Yoga, English translation by Swami Venkatesananda, 1993.

Viveka Chudamani by Shri Sankaracharya, English translation by Shri Jnanananda Bharathi, First Edition.

Books on SHIRDI SAI BABA

ERLINGE

NEW BOOKS

2019-2020

COFFEE TABLE BOOK

New Findings on Shridi Sai Baba
CHANDRABHANU SATPATHY
978 93 86245 52 6
5.5"×8.5"
222pp
Paperback ₹ 300

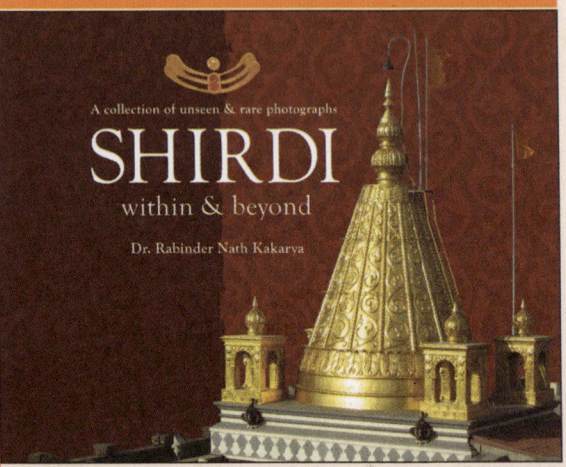

Shirdi Sai Baba is a household name in India as well as in many parts of the World today. Sterling Publishers are well known for publishing the largest number of books on Shirdi Sai, indeed far more than any other publisher. We endeavour to be comprehensive in the range of author and content. We also publish books on other saints and masters.

शिरडी साईं बाबा नवीन तथ्य
चन्द्रभानु सतपथी
978 93 86245 63 2
5.5"×8.5"
224pp
Paperback ₹ 300

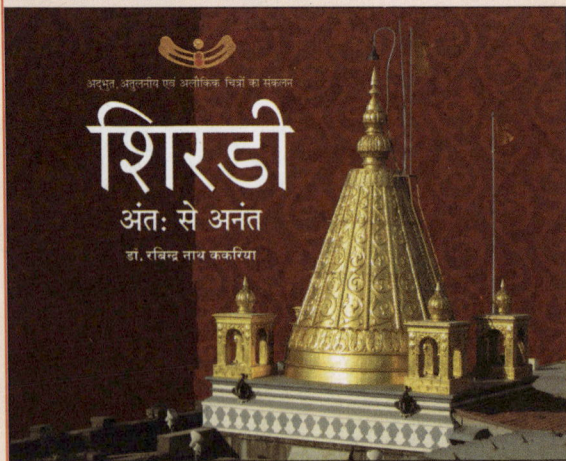

SHIRDI : within & beyond
A collection of unseen & rare photographs
Dr. Rabinder Nath Kakarya
978 81 207 7806 1   ₹ 750

शिरडी अंत: से अनंत
डॉ. रबिन्द्रनाथ ककरिया
978 81 207 8191 7
₹ 750

STERLING

mail@sterlingpublishers.in

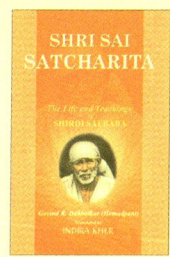

Shri Sai Satcharita
The Life and Teachings of Shirdi Sai Baba
Translated by Indira Kher
ISBN 978 81 207 2211 8
₹ 550(HB)
ISBN 978 81 207 2153 1
₹ 450(PB)

Shirdi Sai Baba: The Universal Master
Sri Kaleshwar
ISBN 978 81 207 9664 5
₹ 150

Shri Sai Ekam Shri Sai is the One
Harjeet Yadav
978 93 86245 38 0
₹ 900

Shri Sai Baba Teachings & Philosophy
Lt Col M B Nimbalkar
ISBN 978 81 207 2364 1
₹ 150

Shirdi Sai Baba
Anusuya Vasudevan
ISBN 978 93 86245 16 8
(64 pages plates)
₹ 200

We need Sai forever... at 6, 16 and 60!
Saurabh Khanna
ISBN 978 93 86245 15 1
₹ 190

Sai Baba of Shirdi: A Biographical Investigation
Kevin R. D. Shepherd
ISBN 978 81 207 9901 1
₹ 450

The Eternal Sai Consciousness
A. R. Nanda
ISBN 978 81 207 9043 8
₹ 200

BABA: The Devotees' Questions
Dr. C. B. Satpathy
ISBN 978 81 207 8966 1
₹ 150

The Loving God: Story of Shirdi Sai Baba
Dr. G. R. Vijayakumar
ISBN 978 81 207 8079 8
₹ 200

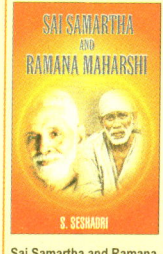

Sai Samartha and Ramana Maharshi
S. Seshadri
ISBN 978 81 207 8986 9
₹150

Shri Sai Gyaneshwari
Rakesh Juneja
ISBN 978 93 86245 05 2
₹ 300

The Age of Shirdi Sai
Dr. C. B. Satpathy
ISBN 978 81 207 8700 1
₹ 300

Message of Shri Sai
Suresh Chandra Panda
ISBN 978 81 207 9512 9
₹ 150

A Divine Journey with Baba
Vinny Chitluri
ISBN 978 81 207 9859 5
₹ 200

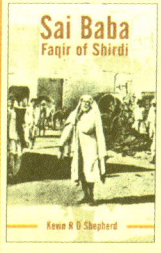

Sai Baba: Faqir of Shirdi
Kevin R.D. Shepherd
ISBN 978 93 86245 06 9
₹ 350

mail@sterlingpublishers.in

STERLING

Baba's Divine Symphony
Vinny Chitluri
ISBN 978 81 207 8485 7
₹ 300

Sai Baba an Incarnation
Bela Sharma
ISBN 978 81 207 8833 6
₹ 200

Shirdi Sai Baba: The Perfect Master
Suresh Chandra Panda & Smita Panda
ISBN 978 81 207 8113 9
₹ 200

The Eternal Sai Phenomenon
A R Nanda
ISBN 978 81 207 6086 8
₹ 200

Baba's Rinanubandh
Leelas during His Sojourn in Shirdi
Compiled by Vinny Chitluri
ISBN 978 81 207 3403 6
₹ 200

Baba's Gurukul SHIRDI
Vinny Chitluri
ISBN 978 81 207 4770 8
₹ 200

Baba's Anurag
Love for His Devotees
Compiled by Vinny Chitluri
ISBN 978 81 207 5447 8
₹ 150

Baba's Vaani: His Sayings and Teachings
Compiled by Vinny Chitluri
ISBN 978 81 207 3859 1
₹ 200

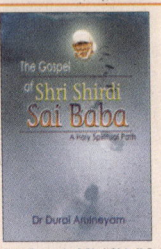
The Gospel of Shri Shirdi Sai Baba: A Holy Spiritual Path
Dr Durai Arulneyam
ISBN 978 81 207 3997 0
₹ 150

Jagat Guru: Shri Shirdi Sai Baba
Prasada Jagannadha Rao
ISBN 978 81 207 8175 7
₹ 100

Spotlight on the Sai Story
Chakor Ajgaonker
ISBN 978 81 207 4399 1
₹ 200

Shirdi Sai Baba A Practical God
K. K. Dixit
ISBN 978 81 207 5918 3
₹ 75

Promises of Shirdi Sai Baba (The Eleven Precious Sayings)
Bela Sharma
ISBN 978 93 85913 98 3
₹ 75

Shirdi Sai Baba The Divine Healer
Raj Chopra
ISBN 978 81 207 4766 1
₹ 150

Shirdi Sai Baba and other Perfect Masters
C B Satpathy
ISBN 978 81 207 2384 9
₹ 150

Sai Hari Katha
Dasganu Maharaj
Translated by
Dr. Rabinder Nath Kakarya
ISBN 978 81 207 3324 4
₹ 100

Unravelling the Enigma: Shirdi Sai Baba in the light of Sufism
Marianne Warren
ISBN 978 81 207 2147 0
₹ 400

I am always with you
Lorraine Walshe-Ryan
ISBN 978 81 207 3192 9
₹ 150

BABA- May I Answer
C.B. Satpathy
ISBN 978 81 207 4594 0
₹ 150

Ek An English Musical on the Life of Shirdi Sai Baba
Usha Akella
ISBN 978 81 207 6842 7
₹ 75

STERLING

mail@sterlingpublishers.in

Sri Sai Baba
Sai Sharan Anand
Translated by V.B Kher
ISBN 978 81 207 1950 7
₹ 200

Sai Baba: His Divine Glimpses
V B Kher
ISBN 978 81 207 2291 0
₹ 95

A Diamond Necklace To: Shirdi Sai Baba
Giridhar Ari
ISBN 978 81 207 5868 1
₹ 200

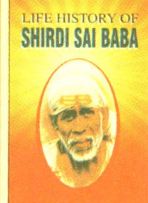
Life History of Shirdi Sai Baba
Ammula Sambasiva Rao
ISBN 978 81 207 7722 4
₹ 225

Shri Sai Baba- The Saviour
Dr. Rabinder Nath Kakarya
ISBN 978 81 207 4701 2
₹ 100

Sai Baba's 261 Leelas
Balkrishna Panday
ISBN 978 81 207 2727 4
₹ 175

A Solemn Pledge from True Tales of Shirdi Sai Baba
Dr B H Briz-Kishore
ISBN 978 81 207 2240 8
₹ 95

God Who Walked on Earth: The Life & Times of Shirdi Sai Baba
Rangaswami Parthasarathy
ISBN 978 81 207 1809 8
₹ 225

Shri Shirdi Sai Baba: His Life and Miracles
ISBN 978 81 207 2877 6
₹ 35

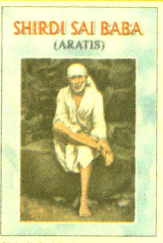
Shirdi Sai Baba Aratis
ISBN 978 81 207 8456 7
(English)
₹ 10

Sree Sai Charitra Darshan
Mohan Jagannath Yadav
ISBN 978 81 207 8346 1
₹ 225

The Miracles of Sai Baba
ISBN 978 81 207 5433 1 (HB)
₹ 300

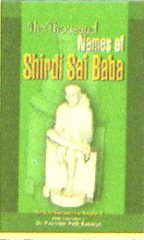
The Thousand Names of Shirdi Sai Baba
Sri B.V. Narasimha Swami Ji
Hindi translation by
Dr. Rabinder Nath Kakarya
ISBN 978 81 207 3738 9
₹ 75

108 Names of Shirdi Sai Baba
ISBN 978 81 207 3074 8
₹ 50

Shirdi Sai Speaks... Sab Ka Malik Ek
Quotes for the Day
ISBN 978 81 207 3101 1
₹ 200

DIVINE GURUS

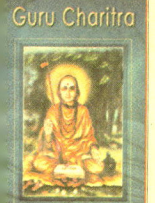
Guru Charitra
Shree Swami Samarth
ISBN 978 81 207 3348 0
₹ 300

Sri Swami Samarth Maharaj of Akkalkot
N.S. Karandikar
ISBN 978 81 207 3445 6
₹ 250

Hazrat Babajan: A Pathan Sufi of Poona
Kevin R. D. Shepherd
ISBN 978 81 207 8698 1
₹ 200

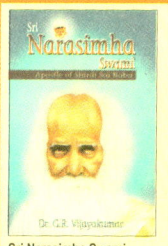
Sri Narasimha Swami Apostle of Shirdi Sai Baba
Dr. G.R. Vijayakumar
ISBN 978 81 207 4432 5
₹ 90

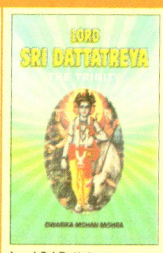
Lord Sri Dattatreya The Trinity
Dwarika Mohan Mishra
ISBN 978 81 207 5417 1
₹ 200

mail@sterlingpublishers.in

STERLING

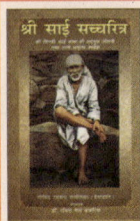
श्री साई सच्चरित्र
श्री शिरडी साई बाबा की अद्भुत जीवनी तथा उनके अमूल्य उपदेश
गोविन्द रघुनाथ दाभोलकर (हेमाडपंत)
978 81 207 2500 3
₹ 350 (HB)

श्री साई ज्ञानेश्वरी- महाकाव्य
राकेश जुनेजा
978 93 86245 17 5
₹ 250

हमें साई की आवश्यकता है सदा के लिए 6, 16 और 60!
सौरभ खत्रा
978 93 86245 21 2
₹ 125

साई ही क्यों?
राकेश जुनेजा
978 81 207 9610 2
₹ 200

जेल में साई साक्षात्कार
राकेश जुनेजा
978 81 207 9507 5
₹ 150

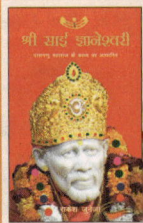
श्री साई ज्ञानेश्वरी
राकेश जुनेजा
978 81 207 9491 7
₹ 250

शिरडी साई बाबा के ग्यारह अनमोल वचन
बेला शर्मा
978 93 85913 97 6
₹ 75

श्री साई चरित्र दर्शन
मोहन जगन्नाथ यादव
978 81 207 8350 8
₹ 200

साई सुमिरन
अंजु टंडन
978 81 207 8706 3
₹ 100

बाबा की वाणी-उनके वचन तथा आदेश
बेला शर्मा
978 81 207 4745 6
₹ 100

बाबा का अनुराग
विनी चितलुरी
978 81 207 6699 0
₹ 125

बाबा का ऋणानुबंध
विनी चितलुरी
978 81 207 5998 5
₹ 150

बाबा का गुरूकुल-शिरडी
विनी चितलुरी
978 81 207 6698 3
₹ 150

बाबा-आध्यात्मिक विचार
चन्द्रभानु सतपथी
978 81 207 4627 5
₹ 175

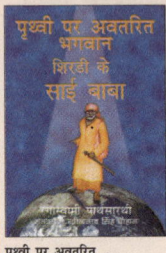
पृथ्वी पर अवतरित भगवान शिरडी के साई बाबा
रंगस्वामी पार्थसारथी
978 81 207 2101 2
₹ 200

साई बाबा एक अवतार
बेला शर्मा
978 81 207 6706 5
₹ 150

साई सत् चरित का प्रकाश
बेला शर्मा
978 81 207 7804 7
₹ 200

श्री शिरडी साई बाबा एवं अन्य सद्गुरु
चन्द्रभानु सतपथी
978 81 207 4401 1
₹ 90

साई शरण में
चन्द्रभानु सतपथी
978 81 207 2802 8
₹ 150

साई - सबका मालिक
कल्पना भाकुनी
978 81 207 9886 1
₹ 200

श्री साई बाबा के परम भक्त
डॉ. रविन्द्रनाथ ककरिया
978 81 207 2779 3
₹ 125

शिरडी अंत: से अनंत
डॉ. रविन्द्रनाथ ककरिया
978 81 207 8191 7
₹ 750

STERLING

mail@sterlingpublishers.in

 श्री साई बाबा के अनन्य भक्त डॉ. रविन्द्र नाथ ककरिया 978 81 207 2705 2 ₹ 100	 साई का संदेश डॉ. रविन्द्र नाथ ककरिया 978 81 207 2879 0 ₹ 200	 श्री साई बाबा के उपदेश व तत्त्वज्ञान लेफ्टिनेन्ट कर्नल एम. बी. निंबालकर 978 81 207 5971 8 ₹ 100	 साई भक्तानुभव डॉ. रविन्द्रनाथ ककरिया 978 81 207 3052 6 ₹ 125	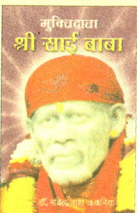 मुक्तिदाता – श्री साई बाबा डॉ. रविन्द्रनाथ ककरिया 978 81 207 2778 6 ₹ 65	 साई दत्तावधूता राजेन्द्र भण्डारी 978 81 207 4400 4 ₹ 75
 साई हरि कथा दासगणु महाराज 978 81 207 3323 7 ₹ 65	 श्री नरसिम्हा स्वामी शिरडी साई बाबा के दिव्य प्रचारक डॉ. रविन्द्र नाथ ककरिया 978 81 207 4437 0 ₹ 100	 शिरडी साई बाबा – की सत्य कथाओं से प्राप्त – एक पावन प्रतिज्ञा प्रो. डॉ. बी.एच. ब्रिज-किशोर 978 81 207 2346 7 ₹ 95	 दिव्य भजन डॉ. रविन्द्रनाथ ककरिया 978 81 207 9505 1 ₹ 125	 शिरडी संपूर्ण दर्शन डॉ. रविन्द्रनाथ ककरिया 978 81 207 2312 2 ₹ 50	 शिरडी साई बाबा की दिव्य लीलाएँ डॉ. रविन्द्र नाथ ककरिया 978 81 207 6376 0 ₹ 150
 श्री साई चालीसा 978 81 207 4773 9 ₹ 50	 शिरडी साई बाबा आरती 978 81 207 8195 5 ₹ 10	 आरती संग्रह (3D cover) on Plastic ISBN 978 81 207 8940 1 Size: 14.20 x 10.70 cm ₹ 60	 आरती संग्रह (Index Boardbook) Gold/Silver Cover ISBN 978 81 207 9057 5 Size: 10.70 x 15.45 cm ₹ 100	 आरती संग्रह (Boardbook) Green Cover ISBN 978 81 207 4774 6 Size: 11 x 15 cm (9 Leafs) ₹ 50	 शिरडी साई के दिव्य वचन-सब का मालिक एक प्रतिदिन का विचार 978 81 207 3533 0 ₹ 200

ORIYA LANGUAGE

 ଶ୍ରୀ ସାଇ ସଚ୍ଚରିତ ଗୋବିନ୍ଦ ରଘୁନାଥ ଦାଭୋଲକର (ହେମାଦପନ୍ତ) 78 81 207 8332 4 300	 ସାଇ ସନ୍ଦେଶ ରବୀନ୍ଦ୍ର ନାଥ କକରିଆ 978 81 207 9534 1 ₹ 100	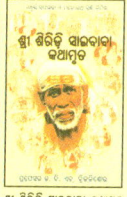 ଶ୍ରୀ ଶିରିଡି ସାଇବାବାଙ୍କ କଥାମୃତ ପୃଥୁରାଜ ଜି. ବି. ସି. ବିଜୁକିଶୋର 978 81 207 7774 0 ₹ 95	 ଶ୍ରୀ ସାଇବାବାଙ୍କ ଉପଦେଶ ଓ ତତ୍ତ୍ୱଜ୍ଞାନ ଏମ. ବି. ନିମ୍ବାଲକର 978 81 207 9982 0 ₹125	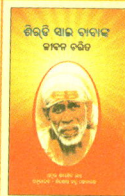 ଶିରିଡି ସାଇ ବାବାଙ୍କ ଜୀବନ ଚରିତ (Oriya) ରବୀନ୍ଦ୍ର ନାଥ କକରିଆ 978 81 207 7417 9 ₹125	

mail@sterlingpublishers.in

STERLING

KANNAD LANGUAGE

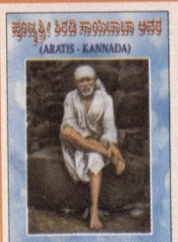
Shirdi Sai Baba Aratis
(Kannada)
₹ 10

ಬಾಬಾದಾ ಸಂತಬಂಧ
ವಿನ್ನಿ ಚಿಟ್ಟಾಬೋರ್
978 81 207 9500 6
₹ 200

ಪೂಜ್ಯ ಶಿರಡಿ ಸಾಯಿಬಾಬಾ ಆವರ
(Kannada)
ಪ್ರೊ. ಡಾ. ಬಿ.ಎಚ್.
ಬ್ರಿಜ್-ಕಿಶೋರ್
978 81 207 2873 8
₹ 95

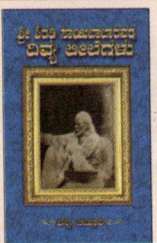
ಶ್ರೀ ಶಿರಡಿ ಸಾಯಿಬಾಬಾರ
ದಿವ್ಯ ಬೋಧನೆ
978 81 207 8930 2
₹ 225

ಬಾಬಾರದೊಂದಿಗೆ ಒಂದು ದಿವ್ಯ
ಪಯಣ
ವಿನ್ನಿ ಚಿಟ್ಟಾಬೋರ್
978 81 207 9975 2
₹ 200

TAMIL AND TELUGU LANGUAGE

MARATHI LANGUAGE

Shirdi Sai Baba Aratis
(Tamil)   ₹ 10

(Tamil)
ಪ್ರೊ. ಡಾ. ಬಿ.ಎಚ್. ಬ್ರಿಜ್-ಕಿಶೋರ್
978 81 207 2876 9   ₹ 95

Shirdi Sai Baba Aratis
(Telugu)   ₹ 10

(Telugu)
ಪ್ರೊ. ಡಾ. ಬಿ.ಎಚ್. ಬ್ರಿಜ್-ಕಿಶೋರ್
978 81 207 2294 1   ₹ 95

शिर्डी साईबाबांची
दिव्य वचने (Marathi)
सबका मालिक एक
दैनंदिन विचार
978 81 207 7518 3
₹ 200

THE THOUSAND NAMES OF GOD

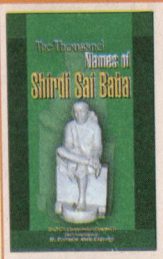
Shirdi Sai Baba
DR. RABINDER NATH KAKARYA
978 81 207 3738 9   ₹75

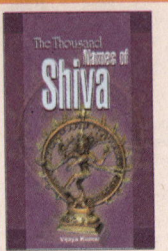
Shiva
VIJAYA KUMAR
978 81 207 3008 3   ₹75

Ganesha
VIJAYA KUMAR
978 81 207 3007 6   ₹75

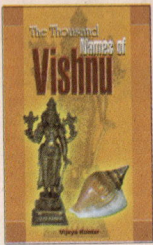
Vishnu
VIJAYA KUMAR
978 81 207 3009 0   ₹75

Colouring My Way
STERLING STUDIO
978 81 207 9790 1   ₹50

108 NAMES OF GOD

Lakshmi
978 81 207 2028 2   ₹50

Shirdi Sai Baba
978 81 207 3074 8   ₹50

Durga
978 81 207 2027 5   ₹50

Shiva
978 81 207 2025 1   ₹50

Hanuman
978 81 207 2024 4   ₹50

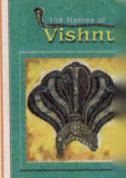
Vishnu
978 81 207 2023 7

Sterling Publishers Private Limited
Plot No. 13, Ecotech-III, Greater Noida - 201306, U. P. India
CIN: U22110DL1964PTC211907 GST: 09AAACS0306C1Z1
Phone No : +91 82877 98380   E-mail : mail@sterlingpublishers.in   www.sterlingpublishers.in